Grammar Upside Down

by Terry Phelps, Ph.D.

Table of Contents

I. Introduction 1
II. Word Functions 2
III. Parts of Speech 4
    A. Nouns 4
    B. Pronouns 5
    C. Adjectives 10
    D. Verbs 14
       1. Tenses 16
         a. Simple 16
         b. Perfect 17
         c. Progressive 17
         d. Regular and Irregular 18
       2. Transitive and Intransitive 21
       3. Active and Passive Voice 22
       4. Mood 23
    E. Adverbs 26
    F. Conjunctions 28
    G. Prepositions 31
    H. Conjunctive Adverbs 34
    I. Transitional Phrases 35
    J. Interjections 35
    K. Parts of Speech P.S. 36
IV. Sentence Patterns 37
    A. Predicate Adjectives 37
    B. Predicate Nominatives 38
    C. Direct Objects 39
    D. Indirect Objects 40
    E. No Complement 41
    F. Commands 41
    G. Questions 43
    H. Compounds 43
       1. Compound Sentence Parts 43
       2. Compound Phrases 43
       3. Compound Sentences 45
    I. Complex Sentences 46
       1. Adjective Clauses 46
       2. Adverb Clauses 47
       3. Noun Clauses 48
V. Verbals 50
    A. Gerunds and Gerund Phrases 50
    B. Participles and Participial Phrases 52
    C. Infinitives and Infinitive Phrases 54
VI. Other Phrases 56
    A. Appositives 56
    B. Absolutes 57
VII. Sentence Options 58
VIII. Parallel Structure 58
IX. Sentence Problems 64
    A. Fragments 64
    B. Comma Splices 66
    C. Fused (Run-on) Sentences 67

    D. Subject-verb Agreement 68
    E. Pronoun-antecedent Agreement 76
    F. Pronoun Case 79
    G. Squinting Modifiers 84
    H. Vague Pronoun Reference 85
    I. Misplaced Modifiers 87
    J. Dangling Modifiers 88
X. Punctuation 90
    A. Commas 90
       1. With Compound Sentences 90
       2. With Introductory Adverb Clauses 91
       3. With Introductory Phrases 91
       4. With Series 94
       5. With Appositives 95
       6. With Nonessential Clauses 95
       7. With Dates and Addresses 96
       8.. With Introductory Expressions 96
       9. With Transition Words 96
       10. With Direct Addresses 96
       11. With Contrasting Phrases 97
       12. With Tag Questions 97
       13. With Omissions 97
       14. With Names and Titles 98
       15. With Parenthetical Comments 98
       16. With Direct Quotations 98
    B. Colons 99
    C. Semi-colons 101
    D. Periods 102
    E. Question Marks 103
    F. Exclamation Points 103
    G. Quotation Marks 105
    H. Parentheses 104
    I. Brackets 105
    J. Slashes 106
    K. Dashes 107
    L. Hyphens 108
    M. Apostrophes 113
       1. Possessives 113
       2. Plurals and Omitted Numbers 117
       3. Contractions 117
XI. Mechanics 119
    A. Capitalization 119
    B. Italics (or Underlining) 120
    C. Numbers (Numerical or Spelled) 121
    D. Ellipsis Marks 123
    E. Abbreviations, Initialisms, Acronyms 124
XII. Clarity Problems 127
XIII. Conciseness 129
XIV. Emphasis 140
XV. Cumulative Sentence for Style, Detail 142
Index 148

Introduction

Why *Grammar Upside Down*?

Most grammar books begin each concept with terminology in a rule or definition, followed by explanation and examples. That abstract-to-concrete approach is often difficult to understand and not memorable. For example, one comma rule will typically read something like this: "Use a comma before the conjunction that connects two independent clauses in a compound sentence." Understanding that rule requires the reader to know what conjunctions, independent clauses, and compound sentence are.

This book is called *Grammar Upside Down* because each concept begins with concrete examples, leading the reader to see word patterns and relationships, and then provides terminology and explanation. This concrete-to-abstract (inductive) approach is much more effective than the usual grammar book approach because we better understand and remember what we figure out for ourselves. Furthermore, the analytical process of figuring out the patterns is the same process we use when applying the patterns in our writing.

Instead of memorizing rules and definitions, you will remember grammar concepts as *Grammar Upside Down* leads you to figure them out for yourself and use them. Remembering terms is less important than developing the analytical skills necessary to make appropriate decisions when writing and revising.

Of course, we must use some terms to communicate – just as musicians, computer programmers, accountants, doctors, and lawyers must have terms. Imagine a doctor in surgery asking a nurse to "hand me one of those long, flat, silver, knife-like things with the sharp little blade," instead of asking for a scalpel. We may never use the terms outside a classroom, but they are useful in moving from one level of understanding to another.

This book builds from the basic functions of words through sentence structures, punctuation, and usage. Then we look at ways to be clearer and more concise, and finally we show how to add emphasis and style to your writing.

As the book leads you to analyze the patterns and relationships, please resist the temptation to skip to the rules and definitions without doing the analyses. The point of *Grammar Upside Down* is to have you analyze and teach yourself.

Word Functions

Understanding grammar means understanding the functions of words and how they relate to each other. Almost every word has one of the following functions:

Naming
Describing
Showing action
Showing being
Connecting

The exceptions are words like *yes, no, please, wow,* and *well,* which will be discussed near the end of the Parts of Speech section of this book.

Notice the function of each word in the following sentences.

1. Most students dislike homework.

Most describes students.
Students names a group of people.
Dislike shows a mental action.
Homework names a thing.

2. She likes opera, but he prefers ballet.

She and he name people.
Opera and ballet name things.
Likes and prefers show action.
But connects the two ideas (She likes opera and he prefers ballet.)

3. Five people in a lifeboat were rescued by the Coast Guard.

People, lifeboat, and Coast Guard all name people or things.
Five describes people.
A describes lifeboat, and the describes Coast Guard.
In and by connect (lifeboat to people and Coast Guard to rescued).
Were rescued shows action.

4. She and I have been friends for several years.

She, I, friends, and years name people or things
Several describes years.
Have been show being.
And connects (she and I), and for connects (years to have been).

5. When the whistle blows, the game is over.

Whistle and game name things.
The describes whistle and over describes game.
Blows shows action.
Is shows being.
When connects (the whistle blows to the game is over).

Because of the placement of words in sentences, figuring out their functions is not always easy. For example, in sentence five above, <u>over</u> describes <u>game</u> but does not come right next to it. Similarly, <u>when</u> connects the two ideas but comes before rather than between them.

Analyze the following sentences and determine the function of each word.

1. Three people bought new homes.

2. Susan is the proud parent of three children.

3. Someone gave me the wrong number.

4. I have no excuse for the absences.

5. Pay me now, or pay me later.

6. My fan stopped working, so I bought a new one.

7. Donna refused payment until she received shipment.

8. Until you stop eating excessively, you will lose no weight.

9. Mr. Dale's greatest difficulty is administering discipline to his pupils.

10. Democracy works in some countries but not in others.

At this point we are going to discuss some terms with which you may or may not already be familiar. Work through the information because it is important practice in analysis.

Nouns

What is the function (naming, describing, showing action, showing being, or connecting) of the underlined words in the following sentences?

> The <u>brick</u> fell off the <u>wall</u>.
> <u>Jeri</u> bought the <u>car</u>.

The underlined words name. **Words that name are called <u>nouns</u> or <u>pronouns</u>.**

We will first consider nouns.

In the sentences above, *brick*, *wall*, *Jeri*, and *car* are things that we can touch, see or detect with our other senses. Most people have no trouble identifying these "concrete" nouns. But other nouns are sometimes more difficult to find – words like *excuse, absences, payment, shipment, difficulty* and *Democracy*. These "abstract" nouns name ideas, acts, feelings, etc.

Perhaps a comparison of concrete and abstract nouns will help. Notice the concrete noun in the first sentence and the abstract noun in the second sentence of each pair of sentences below:

> My <u>watch</u> didn't work.
> My <u>excuse</u> didn't work.
>
> Her <u>make-up</u> was obvious.
> Her <u>confusion</u> was obvious.

Noun Signals

Nouns are sometimes easy to find because of signals.

In the sentence below, what word do you find in front of the nouns *dog*, *man*, and *sidewalk*?

> The dog barked at the man on the sidewalk.

Anytime you see <u>the</u>, a naming word (often a noun) will soon follow.

What similar signals can you find before the nouns *person, hope, argument, airplane, clearance*, and *departure* in the sentences below?

> A <u>person</u> hasn't a <u>hope</u> in an <u>argument</u> with him.
> An <u>airplane</u> must have a <u>clearance</u> before a <u>departure</u>.

A and *an* also signal nouns. *A, an,* and *the* are called <u>articles</u>.

Do articles always appear immediately next to the noun? Notice the articles' locations in relation to the underlined nouns in the following sentences.

> The old <u>man</u> asked for a little <u>help</u> from the young <u>cashier</u>.
> An eager <u>student</u> can make a big <u>impression</u> on a new <u>teacher</u>.

As you can see above, descriptive words sometimes come between articles and nouns.
Find the nouns in the sentences below.

>   A simple answer may be the best possible answer.
>   In the far corner of the wheat field sat an old, rusty tractor.

The nouns signaled by *a, an,* and *the* are *answer, answer, corner, field,* and *tractor.*

Try to find another kind of signal for the underlined nouns in the sentences below.

>   Our <u>lizard</u> shed its <u>skin</u>.
>   Bob's <u>bicycle</u> is parked next to Susan's <u>car</u> in their <u>garage</u>.

Possessive words like *our, its, Bob's, Susan's,* and *their* often signal coming nouns.

Besides signal words, nouns are sometimes easy to find because of their form.
What similarities do you see within the groups of nouns below?

>   a. psychology, sociology, theology, apology
>   b. similarity, hospitality, insanity, serendipity
>   c. motion, agitation, obligation, complication
>   d. feminist, egotist, atheist, realist
>   e. amusement, sentiment, shipment, compliment

Notice that suffixes like *-ology, -ity, -tion, -ist* (or *-ism*), and *-ment* are common among nouns. These signals are especially useful in finding abstract nouns.
Remember, articles, possessives, and suffixes are three signals to keep in mind when looking for nouns.

Practice

Find the nouns in the sentences below:

1. The wrecking crew destroyed the building in thirty minutes.
2. His attitude needs an adjustment.
3. A rolling stone gathers no moss.
4. A dream is a wish your heart makes.
5. Rick's greatest difficulty is accepting criticism.
6. In three weeks your work should be finished.
7. Bob searched the house for his keys.
8. The oldest institution in our town is the corner bank.
9. Her favorite course in college was geology.
10. Imitation is the greatest form of flattery.

Pronouns

How would you most likely say the following sentence instead of the way it is written?

>   John failed John's physical because John had a heart murmur.

Most of us would substitute <u>his</u> and <u>he</u> for <u>John's</u> and the second <u>John</u>: John failed his physical because he had a heart murmur. Pronouns often prevent very noticeable repetition.

Words that take the place of nouns are called <u>pronouns</u>. The word replaced by the pronoun is called its <u>antecedent</u>.

Following is a list of pronouns:

all	another	any	anybody	anyone
anything	each	either	everybody	everyone
everything	few	he	her	hers
him	himself	his	I	it
its	itself	many	me	mine
more	most	much	my	myself
neither	nobody	none	no one	nothing
one	oneself	other	others	our
ours	ourselves	she	some	somebody
someone	something	that	them	themselves
these	their	theirs	they	this
those	us	we	what	whatever
which	whichever	who	whoever	whom
whomever	whose	you	your	yours
yourself				

Remembering pronouns is easier when they are divided into smaller groups. Let's consider the different types of pronouns.

Personal Pronouns

What do *I, me, we, us, you, he, him, she, her, they,* and *them* have in common? In other words, to what kind of nouns do they refer?

They all refer to persons. **Pronouns that refer to people are called <u>personal</u> pronouns. The word *it* is also traditionally considered a personal pronoun.** (The possessive form of *it*, like other personal pronouns, is discussed below.) To help remember personal pronouns, instead of memorizing, find them in the following sentences.

Eric said he plans to see you and me at six.
She asked him to show her the way to the museum.
When the rooster crowed, it awakened us before we wanted to get up.
I don't understand the problems; can you help me with them?

Pronouns in the sentences above are *he, you, me, she, him, her, it, us, we, I, you, me,* and *them.*

Here are other forms of personal pronouns: *her, hers, his, their, theirs, our, ours, your, yours, my, mine,* and *its.* What do they have in common besides referring to persons?

They all show possession, so they are called <u>personal possessive</u> pronouns. To help remember them, find the personal possessive pronouns in the sentences below.

His mother traded her old car for a new one.
Hey Alan, your locker is right next to hers and mine.
In their attic John found his childhood toys in a dusty, old trunk.
Our teacher suggested, "If any of the papers are yours, pick them up."
My tooth was gone; in its place was a dollar bill.

Personal possessive pronouns in the sentences above are *his, her, your, hers, mine, their, his, our, yours, my,* and *its.* Notice that they do not have apostrophes. **Personal possessive pronouns do not use apostrophes.**

Notice that personal possessive pronouns often describe. For example, *his* describes *mother, your* describes *locker,* and *their* describes *attic.* When pronouns describe, they act as adjectives, which will be discussed after pronouns. Remember, as you continue through the groups of pronouns, the purpose is to help remember pronouns by seeing patterns of use.

Demonstrative Pronouns

What do the pronouns *that, this, these,* and *those* do in the following sentences?

> <u>That</u> is the car I want.
> <u>This</u> is the only part of the book I don't understand.
> <u>These</u> are the pictures I wanted.
> <u>Those</u> are the ugliest insects I've ever seen.

The four pronouns point out nouns: *car, part, pictures,* and *insects.*

That, this, these, **and** ***those*** **are called** <u>**demonstrative**</u> **pronouns when they point out.** Notice the demonstrative pronouns in the sentences below.

> You'll never ride <u>that</u> horse.
> <u>This</u> book is just the book I've been seeking.
> <u>These</u> years have been the best of my life.
> You'd better polish <u>those</u> shoes.

In these sentences the demonstrative pronouns *that, this, these,* and *those* describe (acting as adjectives, which will be discussed after pronouns). Like personal possessive pronouns, demonstrative pronouns may also be considered descriptive.

Interrogative Pronouns

What does *who* do in the following sentence?

> Who is she?

Who begins a question. ***Which, who, whom, whose,*** **and** ***what*** **are called** <u>**interrogative**</u> **pronouns when they introduce questions.** Notice the interrogative pronouns in the following sentences.

> Pointing to the muddy footprints, she asked, "<u>Whose</u> are these?"
> <u>Who</u> will be the next cabinet member.
> <u>What</u> are you doing next Friday night?
> With <u>whom</u> did you work?
> <u>Which</u> is your favorite, raspberry or lime sherbet?

Indefinite Pronouns

Do all pronouns take the place of nouns or pronouns? Look at the pronouns in the following sentences. What, if anything, are they replacing?

> Does <u>anyone</u> know what time it is?
> <u>Nobody</u> knows the trouble I've seen.
> <u>One</u> should avoid undeserved criticism.

In the sentences above, *anyone, nobody,* and *one* do not take the place of nouns.

The pronouns *anybody, anyone, anything, everybody, everyone, everything, somebody, someone, something, nobody, no one, nothing,* and *one* are called <u>indefinite</u> pronouns because they do not refer to particular persons or things.

In the following sentence, how many tacks were not found, and how many people like chocolate?
> *Some* of the tacks were never found.
> *Most* people like chocolate.

It is impossible to tell how many because *some* and *most* are not specific numbers. **When *all, another, any, each, either, few, many, more, most, much, neither, none, other, others, several,* and *some* do not indicate a specific number or refer to nonspecific persons or things, they are called <u>indefinite</u> pronouns.**

Find the indefinite pronouns in the following sentences.
> If anybody can do the job, Jeff can.
> Most of us have someone to visit during the holidays.
> I doubt if either of them heard anything you said.
> All of them are ambitious, each in his own way.
> Everybody enjoyed the party so much that we agreed to have another.
> Anybody can find something positive if he or she tries.
> I don't have many, but a few are better than none.

Relative Pronouns

What is the function of the italicized pronouns in the following sentences?
> He met the donor *who* <u>regularly gave a thousand dollars or more</u>.
> No one knew *that* <u>he was so generous</u>.
> Santa came down the chimney, *which* <u>surprised everyone</u>.
> He wasn't the visitor *whom* <u>we all expected</u>.
> It wasn't anyone I know *whose* <u>car was damaged</u>.

Notice that the italicized pronouns connect or relate the underlined group of words to the first part of the sentence. These groups of words are called *clauses,* which will be discussed further in a later section on sentence patterns. **Pronouns that connect clauses are called <u>relative</u> pronouns, including *who, whom, whose, which,* and *that.*** Of course, as noted earlier, *who, whom, whose,* and *which* may be used sometimes as interrogative pronouns, and *that* may be used as a demonstrative pronoun. Either way, they are pronouns.

Indefinite Relative Pronouns

One more group of pronouns, sometimes not categorized in grammar books, is demonstrated in the sentences below.
> <u>Whatever</u> you think, you should speak up.
> <u>Whoever</u> speaks up will be heard.
> You can buy <u>whichever</u> you prefer.
> You can vote for <u>whomever</u> you choose.
> Most people believe <u>what</u> he says.

Notice that the italicized pronouns above introduce ideas (called clauses) and relate them to the rest of the sentence. **When the pronouns *whatever, whoever, whichever, whomever,* or *what* introduce clauses, they are called <u>indefinite relative</u> pronouns.**

Intensive and Reflective Pronouns

(Note: The distinction between intensive and reflexive is generally not important because the main reason for grouping/labeling pronouns is to help remember the large number of pronouns. But the difference between intensive and reflexive is shown below.)

Why would someone include the underlined words in the following sentences? To what preceding word in each sentence is the underlined word referring?

> I did it <u>myself</u>.
> The students did the work <u>themselves</u>.
> The dean <u>herself</u> wrote Janice a thank you letter.

In the sentences above, *myself* refers to *I*, *themselves* refers to *students*, and *herself* refers to *dean*. We often use these pronouns to emphasize separateness. Each underlined pronoun in the sentences above refers to the subject of that sentence. **The pronouns *myself*, *ourselves*, *yourself*, *yourselves*, *himself*, *herself*, *themselves*, and *itself* are called <u>intensive</u> when they emphasize the subject.**

The same pronouns may be called "reflexive" when used as in the sentences below.

> He hurt <u>himself</u> while skiing.
> She asked <u>herself</u>, "What am I doing here?"
> The debaters argued among <u>themselves</u> for practice.

In the sentences above, *Himself* receives the action of *hurt* and is called a "direct object" (see Sentence Pattern 3 in a later section). *Herself* receives the action of *asked* and is called an "indirect object" (see Sentence Pattern 4 in a later section). *Themselves* is an "object of a preposition" *among* (see Prepositions later in this section on Parts of Speech). **When pronouns with suffixes *-self* or *-selves* are used as objects, they are called <u>reflexive</u>.**

Reciprocal Pronouns

One last category of pronouns is shown in the following sentences:

> We gave <u>each other</u> gifts for Christmas.
> I believe that we should love <u>one another</u> as we love ourselves.
> The dogs sniffed <u>each other</u>.

Each other and *one another* are called <u>reciprocal pronouns</u>, **which indicate a mutual action or relationship between two or more people or things.**

Notice that reciprocal pronouns may be possessive, as in the following sentence:

> Jack and Jill understood <u>each other's</u> suggestions to solve the problem.

Why recognize different kinds of pronouns?
As noted earlier, one purpose of grouping pronouns as personal, personal possessive, demonstrative, interrogative, relative, indefinite, reflexive, intensive, and reciprocal helps is to help remember all the pronouns, not the terminology. Being able to recognize pronouns will be useful in fixing problems such as pronoun case and pronoun-antecedent agreement, discussed in later sections.

Practice
Pronouns are mixed in the following sentences. See if you can find them all.
1. Someone needs to speak with him about the problem.

2. I am learning to use a computer, and it is really interesting.
3. This is the book I mentioned to you.
4. Whose idea was it to cancel those subscriptions?
5. My main question was, "What are the chances of success?"
6. He will work himself to death if we let him.
7. Do unto others as you would have them do unto you.
8. Many may die before anything is done to stop its spread.
9. I would rather do it myself if nobody objects.
10. All of the students did something to help meet the deadline.
11. Surprisingly, neither of them completed many of the problems.
12. Whatever he said offended everyone in the room.
13. I'd like to talk with whoever wrote that article.
14. They gave each other dirty looks.

Adjectives

Recalling the five functions of words (naming, describing, showing action or being, connecting), determine the function of the underlined words in the sentences below.

>His den was a <u>musty</u>, <u>dark</u> room.

>**<u>Three</u>** candles burned in the <u>open</u> window.

>The <u>youngest</u> son was a whiz in math.

>**<u>Four</u>** others waited in the <u>reception</u> room.

The underlined words describe. What kinds of words do they describe? What do they tell or what questions do they answer about the words they describe?

All but one of the underlined words describe nouns (*room, candles, window, son,* and *room).* The other underlined word describes a pronoun (*others*). They tell <u>what kind</u> of room (*musty, dark*), <u>how many</u> candles (*three* and *four*), and <u>which</u> boy (*youngest*).
Words that describe nouns or pronouns are called <u>adjectives</u>, and they tell three things about nouns or pronouns: which one, what kind, or how many.
In other words, if we can name something, we can describe it, and the words we use to describe nouns and pronouns are adjectives. The English language includes thousands of adjectives.

There are three special kinds of adjectives we may not recognize as adjectives.
What do the possessive nouns and pronouns do in the sentence below?

>**<u>John's</u>** bike was in <u>his</u> garage.

John's describes the noun *bike,* and *his* describes the noun *garage*. Therefore, *John's* and *his* are used as adjectives. Possessive nouns and pronouns are frequently used as adjectives.
Often a word may have different functions in different sentences. Notice the different uses of the underlined words in the following sentences:

>**<u>Apple</u>** pie is my favorite <u>dessert</u> dish.

>He ate an <u>apple</u> for <u>dessert</u>.

>**<u>Some</u>** are lazy, but <u>most</u> work hard.

>**<u>Some</u>** problems are difficult, but <u>most</u> students can get them.

Apple and *dessert* are used as adjectives in the first sentence and as nouns in the second.
Some and *most* are used as pronouns in one sentence and as adjectives in the other.

Articles *a*, *an*, and *the*, mentioned earlier as signals for nouns, are also considered adjectives.

So far, all the adjectives have been in front of the words they describe. Is this always the location of adjectives? Analyze the sentences below. Where are the adjectives located?

> My sister is <u>brilliant</u>, but my brother is <u>average</u>.
> The wind, <u>strong</u> and <u>gusty</u>, made his kite <u>crazy</u>.

Notice that *brilliant, average, strong, gusty,* and *crazy* all follow somewhere after the words they describe.

Practice
Find the adjectives and the nouns and pronouns they are describing in the following sentences.
1. The weary old man sat down in the wicker chair.
2. My new laptop computer is almost as light as my tablet.
3. Every college student has experienced the hassles of enrolling.
4. Five children ran through my aunt's petunia bed.
5. A strawberry lollipop will keep my sister happy.
6. The wound, red and swollen, required a doctor's care.
7. Surely you aren't going to buy that yellow shag carpet.
8. His little sister looks angelic, but she is demonic.
9. A huge fire engulfed the entire building in thirty minutes.

Comparative and Superlative Adjectives

Comparative and superlative adjectives compare, with slight variations. Here are some examples.

> Jan is happy.
> Jan is happier than Joe. (comparative)
> Jan is happiest of all the students. (superlative)

Let's examine the differences between comparative and superlative adjectives.

Comparative

What is the difference between the uses of underlined adjectives in the following sentences?

> Sara is <u>smart</u>.
> Sara is <u>smarter</u> than Brad.

In the first sentence above, *smart* merely describes *Sara*; in the second sentence *smarter* describes *Sara* in comparison with *Brad*. Notice the similar pattern in the pairs of sentences below.

> Granny Bryce is <u>old</u>.
> Her <u>older</u> sister is 99.

> This pork is <u>lean</u>.
> A <u>leaner</u> meat is chicken.

The apartment at Oak Ridge was a <u>great</u> deal.
Living rent-free at home with my family was a <u>greater</u> deal.

To indicate a comparison of <u>two</u> things, most one-syllable adjectives add *-er*. This is the <u>comparative</u> degree, indicating a greater or lesser degree in one thing than in another.

There are a few exceptions with one-syllable adjectives that do not add *–er,* as shown in sentences below.
Lunch was <u>good</u>.
Dinner was <u>better</u>

He doesn't feel <u>well</u>.
He feels <u>more well</u> than yesterday.

The weather looks <u>bad</u>.
The weather looks <u>worse</u> than yesterday.

What about two-syllable adjectives? Do all two-syllable adjectives also add *-er* for the comparative degree? Look at the sentences below.
He's <u>mellower</u> after a session of yoga.
Geometry is <u>simpler</u> than calculus.
Nicole Kidman became <u>more famous</u> after the divorce.
Please be <u>more careful</u> on your next trip.

Obviously, some two-syllable adjectives like *mellow* and *simple* add *-er* (or *r* if they already end in *e* as in *simple*), and others like *famous* and *careful* do not. We wouldn't say *famouser* and *carefuler* but instead we add *more.* **Some two-syllable adjectives add *-er*, and others instead require *more* to show the comparative degree.**

Is there any consistent pattern? Actually, there are a few that may not have exceptions. Look at the pairs below:
crazy   crazier
silly   sillier
happy   happier
easy   easier
pretty   prettier

With two-syllable adjectives ending in *y,* we generally change the *y* to *i* and then add *-er.*
What do you notice about the comparative adjectives below with three or more syllables?
Friendship is <u>more important</u> than possessions.
She is <u>more professional</u> than he is.
Adjectives of three or more syllables are made comparative by adding *more.*

Below is another pattern with participles (verbs used as adjectives). What do these comparative participles—whether present (*-ed*) or past (*-ing*) have in common?
He seemed <u>more amused</u> by the sequel than the original movie.
I've never seen a <u>more sheltered</u> child.
It was <u>more frustrating</u> than walking on ice.
His directions were <u>more confusing</u> than the map.

Participles used as adjectives require *more* to show the comparative degree. Adding an *-er* doesn't work as you can see with these non-words: *amuseder, sheltereder, frustratinger, confusinger.*

Superlative

Compare the forms of underlined adjectives in the pairs of sentences below:

> The first movie was the <u>scarier</u> of the double feature.
> The first movie was the <u>scariest</u> of the series of films.
>
> Of the two brothers, John is the <u>more studious</u>.
> Of all the students in the class, John is the <u>most studious</u>.

In the first sentence of each pair above, two things are compared; therefore, the comparative degree is appropriate: *scarier* and *more studious*. The second sentence of each pair compares more than two things, using the superlative degree. **Adjectives comparing more than two things indicate the superlative (or greatest) degree and either end in *-est* or are preceded by *most*.**

Looking at the previous discussion of when to use *-er* or *more* for comparative degree, would you expect similar patterns for using *-est* and *most* for superlative degree? For example, in the following sentences, compare the patterns:

One-syllable adjectives

> She is <u>old</u>.
> Her brother is <u>older</u> than she.
> Her sister is the <u>oldest</u> of the three.

Two-syllable adjectives

> Calculus is <u>simple</u>.
> Geometry is <u>simpler</u>.
> Algebra is <u>simplest</u> of the three advanced math courses.
> Jack was <u>careful</u> with his words.
> Jill was <u>more careful</u> with her words than Jack.
> Jane was the <u>most careful</u> of the group.

Adjectives with more than two syllables

> The first test was <u>difficult</u>.
> The second test was <u>more difficult</u>.
> The third test was the <u>most difficult</u> of all.

When the comparative adjective ends in *-er*, the superlative ends in *-est*, and when the comparative is preceded by *more*, the superlative is preceded by *most*.

Common Error – Superlative for Comparison of Two

In everyday speech, people frequently use the superlative even in comparing two things, so they might say, "The first movie was the scariest of the double feature," and "Of the two brothers, John is the most studious." **Using the superlative to compare two things is nonstandard English.** In other words, for communication that requires Standard English (e.g., academic or professional writing), use *-est* or *most* <u>only</u> for the superlative degree, <u>not</u> for the comparative degree.

Less Common Error

Occasionally you may hear a doubling of *-er* with *more* or a doubling of *-est* with *most,* as in "She has not been more happier since then." This is nonstandard.

Exception

The following sentences appear to be exceptions to the patterns discussed above. Even though each sentence compares more than two things, the comparative form is used. Why would the superlative form not work in these sentences?

> The elm is <u>taller</u> than all our other trees.
> She is <u>more reliable</u> than her siblings.

We wouldn't say "is tallest than" or "is most reliable than" because the conjunction *than* sets up a comparison of one thing (*elm* or *she* in the above sentences) with a group (*trees* or *siblings*) rather than comparing one thing to two or more individual things. Therefore, **when a comparison involves *than,* use the comparative form of the adjective.** Notice how this works even in a comparison such as the following:

> He has <u>better</u> manners than his brothers.

In the above sentence *better* compares the *manners* of one brother to the other brothers as a group.

Verbs

Recalling the five functions of words (naming, describing, showing action or being, connecting), determine what the underlined words do in the sentences below.

> The *Challenger* <u>landed</u> at Edwards AFB.
> Sutton <u>hurled</u> the ball to the plate.
> She <u>sniffed</u> the casserole.
> The dog <u>bit</u> me.
> The committee <u>listened</u> to testimony for three days.

If you said the underlined words show action, you are right.
Words that show action are called <u>verbs.</u>
The actions in the sentences above (*landed, hurled, sniffed, bit,* and *listened*) are physical. Are all actions physical?

Determine the function of the underlined words below.

> I <u>trust</u> you completely because you never break your word.
> We <u>understand</u> the importance of the report.
> Lillee <u>thought</u> the song was beautiful.
> Carolyn <u>remembered</u> the appointment just in time.
> Avery <u>likes</u> dark chocolate the best.
> Teryn <u>forgave</u> the bully when he sincerely apologized.
> Her speech <u>impressed</u> everyone.
> They <u>prefer</u> hamburgers over hotdogs.
> He <u>wanted</u> a career in acting.
> I <u>have</u> three dollars.
> Our landlord <u>owns</u> three buildings.

The underlined words above are all actions but not physical. Actions may be mental acts – preferences, choices, thoughts, desires, etc.

Find the verbs in the following sentences. Some are physical actions, and some are not physical.

> The cat stretched and yawned.
> The car squealed around the corner.
> We rested for a few minutes then resumed our game.
> The chronometer indicated twelve, and the rodent descended.
> The touchdown tied the game and sent it into overtime.
> My line broke, so the fish escaped.
> He gained thirty pounds last summer and bought a new wardrobe.

The action verbs in the sentences above are *stretched, yawned, squealed, rested, resumed, indicated, descended, tied, sent, broke, escaped, gained* and *bought.*

All complete sentences contain verbs. With action verbs, someone or something is <u>doing</u> something. But not all sentences involve action. Notice the underlined verbs below:

> I <u>am</u> positive about the date.
> They <u>were</u> constant companions for thirty years.
> When Gavin <u>was</u> three, his favorite toy <u>was</u> a drum.

Some sentences merely talk about someone or something <u>being</u> something.
Words that show <u>being</u> or <u>perception</u> or <u>relationship</u> also called <u>being</u> or <u>stative</u> verbs.

Find the <u>being</u> verbs in the sentences below.

> We were a few minutes late, but she was not angry.
> These are the most difficult problems in the assignment.
> This is her last attempt at an Olympic medal.
> I am an only child.

All the verbs above (*were, was, are, is,* and *am*) are forms of *be.*

What is the difference between the verbs in the sentences below?

> Seattle <u>was</u> her destination.
> Seattle <u>will be</u> her destination.

The first sentence refers to the past and the second to the future. That time difference is indicated by the form of *be.* Sometimes the forms require helping verbs such as *will.*

Helping verbs have other uses besides showing time. What difference do the helping verbs make below?

> Leah <u>will be</u> angry.
> Leah <u>might be</u> angry.

<u>Will be</u> is definite; <u>might be</u> is uncertain. Similarly, <u>could be</u>, <u>should be</u>, and <u>may be</u> indicate varying degrees of certainty. Notice in the following sentence that the *being* verb includes two helping verbs.

> Leah <u>might have been</u> angry.

If *being* verbs can include helpers, what about *action verbs*? Look at the sentences below.

> Larry <u>could have gone</u> to Paris if he <u>had drawn</u> the lucky number.
> She <u>has tried</u> everything, but nothing <u>will remove</u> the stain.

We <u>were told</u> you <u>might be looking</u> for new employees.

Davis <u>could have been injured</u> more seriously.

Action verbs can have helpers for the same reasons as being verbs. You may have noticed that forms of *be* (*were*, *be*, and *been*) are used as helping verbs in the third and fourth sentences above. **Verbs with helping verbs are called <u>verb phrases.</u>**

Look at the arrangement of verb phrases in the following sentences.

<u>Can</u> you <u>help</u> me with this sentence?

He <u>did</u> not <u>understand</u> the problem.

<u>Will</u> you ever <u>see</u> that movie?

Notice in the sentences above that verb phrases can be interrupted by other words. Sentence structure varies for questions and negating words like *not*. Verb phrases are one factor in verb tenses, which are discussed in below in Verb Tenses.

Practice

Locate the verbs and verb phrases in the following sentences. Some sentences have more than one.

1. We found the envelope in the top drawer.
2. They will be looking for us when the sun goes down.
3. People can be funny sometimes.
4. You are the committee's first choice.
5. Where did you get that dress?
6. Someone misinformed you about the time.
7. Please leave your name and number at the sound of the tone.
8. This might have been his last performance.
9. No one is sure of his name, but we were told it is Dale.
10. She said she had no problem with geometry, but algebra gave her fits.
11. I believe the children are our future; teach them well and let them lead.
12. The governor strongly endorsed the bill, but he hesitated to publicize it.
13. She will get elected if the voters understand her platform.

Verb Tenses

<u>Simple Tenses</u>

Notice the times and the forms of the verbs indicated in the sentences below.

Today I <u>work</u>.

Yesterday I <u>worked</u>.

Tomorrow I <u>will work</u>.

Today I <u>am</u> happy.

Yesterday I <u>was</u> happy.

Tomorrow I <u>will be</u> happy.

Verb tenses indicate when something happens/happened (action verbs) or exists/existed (being verbs).

Basically, verb tenses indicate present, past, and future, as shown above with *work* and *am* (present), *worked* and *was* (past), and *will work* and *will be* (future). These are called <u>simple tenses</u>. **Simple verb tenses are present, past, and future.**

Verb tenses get more complicated with Perfect Tenses, Progressive Tenses, Regular and Irregular Verbs, and Moods, as you will see in the next several pages.

Perfect Tenses

To indicate more precise times, we use helping verbs (also called "auxiliary verbs") such as *will* in the sentences above. Notice the times and forms of verbs indicated in the sentences below.
1. I <u>have worked</u> all day.
2. I <u>had worked</u> for two hours before lunch.
3. Next week I <u>will have worked</u> for this company for two years.

The verb forms above, called <u>perfect tenses</u>, indicate that something happened or existed before other actions or conditions. Again, notice the helping verbs that indicate the tense: *have, had,* and *will have.*

In sentence #1 above, **the verb indicates an action begun in the past and continuing into the present. This is call present perfect tense.**

In sentence #2 above, **the verb indicates an action that took place before something else in the past. This is call <u>past perfect</u> tense.**

In sentence #3 above, **the verb indicates that an action will be <u>finished</u> in the future. This is called <u>future perfect</u> tense.**

Progressive Tenses

Notice the differences among the verb forms below.
1. I <u>am working.</u>
2. I <u>was working</u> when she called.
3. I <u>will be working</u> Saturday.
4. I <u>have been working</u> since noon.
5. I <u>had been working</u> before you called.
6. I <u>will have been working</u> here for two years in January.

In sentence #1 above, **the verb indicates continuing action in the present. This is called present progressive tense.**

In sentence #2 **the verb indicates a continuing action in the past. This is called past progressive tense.**

In sentence #3 **the verb indicates a continuing action in the future. This is called future progressive tense.**

In sentence #4 **the verb indicates a continuing action from the past to the present. This is called present perfect progressive tense.**

In sentence #5 **the verb indicates a continuing action in the past before another action in the past. This is called past perfect progressive tense.**

In sentence #6 **the verb indicates an action that will continue to a definite time in the future. This is called future perfect progressive tense.**

The terminology of all the tenses is not so important, but using the appropriate tense helps communicate precise time.

Regular and Irregular Verbs

Look at the verbs below and compare the patterns.

Present	Past	Past Participle
I walk.	I walked.	I have walked.
You like.	You liked.	You have liked.
She looks.	She looked.	She has looked .

Notice that the past and past participles above are all formed by adding *d* or *ed*.
Verbs that form past and past participle by adding *d* or *ed* are called *regular* verbs.

You may also have noticed that the past participle form has a helping verb. Do past participle verbs always use *has* or *have?* Examine those below.

John was fired.   They had walked.
We were warned.   She has been accepted.

Helping verbs may vary with past participles.

What do you notice about the pattern of tenses in the verbs below, different from the tenses above (such as *walk, walked,* and *have walked*)?

Present	Past	Past Participle
I eat.	I ate.	I have eaten.
You sing.	You sang.	You have sung.
He brings.	He brought.	He has brought.

Notice the absence of a consistent pattern in the verbs above. **Verbs that form past and past participles in ways different from adding *d* or *ed* are called *irregular.***

Below are the standard forms of past and past participle for the irregular verbs.

Present	Past	Past Participle	Present	Past	Past Participle
arise	arose	arisen	awake	awoke/awaked	awoke/awaked
be	was/were	been	beat	beat	beaten
become	became	become	begin	began	begun
bend	bent	bent	bite	bit	bitten
blow	blew	blown	break	broke	broken
bring	brought	brought	build	built	built
burst	burst	burst	buy	bought	bought
buy	bought	bought	catch	caught	caught
choose	chose	chosen	cling	clung	clung
come	came	come	cost	cost	cost
deal	dealt	dealt	dig	dug	dug
dive	dived/dove	dived	do	did	done

draw	drew	drawn	dream	dreamt/dreamed	dreamt/dreamed
drink	drank	drunk	drive	drove	driven
eat	ate	eaten	fall	fell	fallen
fight	fought	fought	find	found	found
fly	flew	flown	forget	forgot	forgotten
freeze	froze	frozen	get	got	gotten
give	gave	given	go	went	gone
grow	grew	grown	hang	hung	hung
have	had	had	hear	heard	heard
hide	hid	hidden	hurt	hurt	hurt
keep	kept	kept	know	knew	known
lay	laid	laid	lead	led	led
lend	lent	lent	let	let	let
lie	lay	lain	lose	lost	lost
make	made	made	prove	proved	proved/proven
read	read	read	ride	Rode	ridden
ring	rang	rung	rise	rose	risen
run	ran	run	say	said	said
see	saw	seen	send	sent	sent
set	set	set	shake	shook	shaken
shoot	shot	shot	shrink	shrank	shrunk
sing	sang	sung	sink	sank	sunk
sit	sat	sat	slay	slew	slain
sleep	slept	slept	speak	spoke	spoken
spin	spun	spun	spring	sprang	sprung
stand	stood	stood	steal	stole	stolen
sting	stung	stung	strike	struck	struck/stricken*
swear	swore	sworn	swim	swam	swam
swing	swung	swung	take	took	taken
teach	taught	taught	throw	threw	thrown
wake	woke/waked	woken/waked	wear	wore	worn
wring	wrung	wrung	write	wrote	written

Notice that options are acceptable for *awake, dive, dream, prove, strike* and *wake*. The regular verb form *awaked* is acceptable for both past and past participle of *awake*, and *awakened* is acceptable for past participle. Either *dived* or *dove* is acceptable for the past tense of dive. Either *dreamt* or *dreamed* is acceptable for the past and past participle of *dream*. Either *proved* or *proven* is acceptable for the past participle of *prove*. Either *woke* or *waked* are acceptable for past and past participle of *wake*.

*The past participle form of *strike* is *struck* except when referring to being *stricken* with a disease, guilt, a wound, misfortune, etc., or when something is *stricken* from a legal document or testimony.

Troublesome Pairs
Two particular pairs of irregular verbs are especially troublesome because people confuse them.

Lie vs. Lay
Compare the forms of *lie* and *lay* below (which include the present participle forms). Why do you think they are sometimes confused?

    Each night I <u>lie</u> under the stars and try to fathom the universe.
    I <u>lay</u> there for an hour, too sore to move.
    The book <u>has lain</u> unopened on her desk since she bought it.
    The cat was <u>lying</u> in wait for the mouse to emerge.

    Please <u>lay</u> your cards on the table.
    The jeweler carefully <u>laid</u> the diamonds on the blue velvet mat.
    The chickens <u>have laid</u> enough eggs to keep us fed for a week.
    He was <u>laying</u> the blame on someone else.

When referring to the act of reclining, *lie, lay, (has) lain* and *lying* are the Standard English verb form, called "intransitive" (discussed below) when the action is just done, not done <u>to</u> anything. However, when referring to the act of placing something (a direct object, such as *eggs* or *blame* above), *lay, laid, (have) laid*, and *laying* are the standard "transitive" verbs (with objects receiving action). Obviously, some confusion arises because the past tense of *lie* is the same word as the present tense of *lay*. Some confusion may also arise from the verb *lie* meaning to tell a lie, which is a regular verb using *lie, lied, (have) lied*, and *lying* as its standard forms. Familiarize yourself with the forms of *lie* and *lay* below.

Present	Past	Past Participle	Present Participle
lay (put)	laid	laid	laying
lie (recline)	lay	lain	lying

Sit vs. Set
Now compare a second troublesome pair, *sit* and *set*. Why do you suppose they are sometimes confused?

    The children *sit* quietly, though perhaps restlessly, during class.
    They *sat* together on the sofa, making goo-goo eyes at each other.
    He complained that he *had sat* for more than an hour waiting for the clerk.

    Please *set* the vase in the window.
    Last week he *set* a record for the mile run.
    Each year the committee *has set* new standards.

In the sentences above, notice that *set* is used exclusively for putting something. (One exception is the sun *setting*.) There is no overlapping between the forms of *sit* and *set*. Familiarize yourself with the forms of *set* and *sit* below.

Present	Past	Past Participle	Present Participle
set	set	set	setting
sit	sat	sat	sitting

Practice
Determine the correct past or past participle form of the underlined verb in each of the following sentences. Some are already correct.

1. He has <u>swim</u> across the English Channel.
2. I understand that the antique desk <u>cost</u> him a fortune.
3. The President claims that it was he who <u>lead</u> us out of the recession.
4. He <u>hurt</u> his chances for selection by not being tactful.
5. For the past week they have <u>ring</u> the bell at dinnertime.
6. Jack has <u>lie</u> in a hospital bed for eight days.
7. He <u>swing</u> at the pitch and <u>strike</u> out.
8. She <u>wear</u> the same dress every day last week for good luck.
9. The wasp <u>sting</u> him on the arm and caused a reaction.
10. When Daylight Savings Time rolls around, be sure to <u>set</u> your clocks back.
11. Yesterday he <u>laid</u> in the sun for two hours and got a nasty sunburn.
12. When you have <u>sit</u> in one position long enough, your bottom conforms to the chair.

Transitive and Intransitive Verbs

Compare the first two sentences below with the next three. Notice that only the verbs in the first two sentences below are <u>done to something.</u>
1. They <u>watched</u> the game.
2. He <u>believed</u> her.
3. She <u>fell</u>.
4. The odor <u>was</u> strong.
5. She <u>is</u> a genius.

Notice that the verbs in the last three sentences above are just done, not done to anything.
Verbs that are actions done to something are called <u>transitive verbs</u>, with something or someone receiving their action. Verbs that are not actions done to something (merely linking or an action without a receiver of the action) are called <u>intransitive verbs.</u>

What do you notice about the verbs below? Are they transitive or intransitive?
  The tree quickly <u>grew</u>.
  The tree <u>grew</u> new branches.
  The temperature <u>dropped</u>.
  My brother <u>dropped</u> the thermometer.
As you can see above, some verbs may be intransitive in some sentences and transitive in others.

Voice – Active and Passive

Compare the two sentences below. Which sounds more direct and emphatic?
  Bonnie hit the ball.
  The ball was hit by Bonnie.

The first sentence has more punch because it is shorter and to the point. Notice that the two sentences have different subjects. What is the subject of the first sentence? Is it doing the action or receiving the action? Answer those same questions about the second sentence.

Bonnie, the subject of the first sentence, is doing the action. *Ball,* the subject of the second sentence, is receiving the action. **When the subject does the action, it is called *active voice.* When the subject receives the action, it is called *passive voice.***

Active voice is generally preferred because of its directness and conciseness. However, you may notice that the previous sentence and the last half of this one are written in passive voice. Why? Is the doer of the action mentioned in either sentence? What does this suggest about one reason for using passive voice?

Sometimes the writer may not know who or what did the action or may prefer not to mention the doer. Then passive voice is preferable. Notice the use of passive voice in the sentences below; what would happen if you changed them to active voice, and how would you do that?
>   1. The bank was robbed.
>   2. Hundreds of suggestions were offered for the new program.

To make sentence #1 active voice would require a subject like *someone* unless the robber's identity was available. The resulting sentence, "Someone robbed the bank," would place emphasis on an indefinite subject, *someone* – probably not the intended point of emphasis. In sentence #2 the subject might be a collective noun like *customers,* so the sentence might read, "Customers offered hundreds of suggestions for the new program." An alternative would be to name all the people who are suggesting – not very practical. In either active voice revision, though, the emphasis changes. Notice also what gets the emphasis in the original sentence #2: "Hundreds of suggestions." Isn't that what the writer wants to emphasize?

Passive voice may be used to omit the doer of the action or to emphasize the receiver of the action.

Of course, the bold-faced sentence above might have been written, "Use passive voice to omit the doer of the action or to emphasize the receiver," using an imperative sentence (command) to omit the doer. However, that sounds like a command instead of an option, and the intention of the writer here was to communicate passive voice as an option.

Incidentally, the previous sentence mentions the *writer.* Sometimes writers use passive voice to avoid using *I* or other references to the writer (which is the case in the first sentence of the previous paragraph as well). This use of passive voice is common in dissertations, legal documents, memos, and various other forms of writing, e.g., "A study was conducted to determine. . ." Another common example of passive voice for anonymity is in the minutes of meetings, e.g., "The meeting was called to order. Minutes were read and approved. . ." **Some forms of writing traditionally use passive voice to make the doer of the action anonymous or to avoid first person (*I*).**

Sometimes people confuse *passive voice* with *past tense.* What is the tense of the following sentences?
>   You will be surprised by the results of the survey.
>   Every day someone is victimized by crime.

Notice that the first sentence above is in future tense, and the second is in present tense. Both are in passive voice. **Passive voice has nothing to do with <u>past</u> tense.**

When attempting to convert passive voice to active voice, the task is to put the doer in the subject position. If the sentence contains no doer, the writer must add the doer if she/he wants active voice. Passive constructions that include the doer have a common pattern as in the sentences below. Where are the doers located in each sentence?
>   Hal was programmed by a genius.
>   The city will be engulfed by a giant tidal wave.
>   Most of the world's resources are consumed by a small number of people.

Notice that the doer of each sentence above is located in a prepositional phrase beginning with *by*. This is a consistent pattern with passive voice. Find the *by* phrase, and you find the doer. Now rewrite the sentences above to move the doers into the subject position, and you'll have active voice.

Practice
In the sentences below, determine if the construction is active or passive voice. If passive, is that preferable? If passive is not preferable for one of the reasons above (emphasis on the receiver, anonymity of the doer), change to active. If you leave a sentence passive, make sure it is for one of those reasons.
1. Ralph Waldo Emerson wrote an enlightening essay on friendship.
2. The book was written by an expert in psychotherapy.
3. Susan is repeatedly awakened by a bizarre dream.
4. No one was informed of the new policy until yesterday.
5. Anything you say may be held against you.
6. Extensive research has been conducted on super conductors.
7. He wasn't given many performing opportunities by his manager.
8. The deposits are always made by the secretary.
9. I wrote a ten-page paper on the history of dance.

Mood – Indicative, Imperative and Subjunctive

The term *mood* is used to discuss three "attitudes" that writers can express through verbs in their sentences, in other words, how they're said. For example, what are the different attitudes in the sentences below?

The first sentence is a statement; the second is a command. The first sentence is called the *indicative mood*. The second is called the *imperative mood*. Let's examine these more closely before we look at a third mood.

Indicative Mood
All the sentences below are indicative. What two things do they do?

> What time is it?
> Heather was late for the appointment.
> This could be his last novel.
> Should we go?

The above sentences either make statements or ask questions. **Indicative mood expresses statements or asks questions.**

Imperative Mood
All the sentences below are imperative. What do they all do?

> Be careful when you drive on ice.
> Please tell me again how much you love me.
> Jack, jump over the candlestick.
> Never walk through Central Park at night.

The sentences above are all commands. **Imperative mood expresses commands.**
Looking back at them, can you find a subject of the command? What is the subject of "be careful," of "tell me," of "jump," and of "never walk"? The subject is often not present in commands but is an understood *you*. Thus, we could say, "You be careful when you drive on ice." Even in the sentence "Jack, jump over the candlestick" the subject is the understood *you; Jack* is the person being addressed (called a "direct address"), not the subject.

Subjunctive Mood

The least familiar mood is subjunctive because it is becoming less common in everyday speech. Besides the verb *were,* what do the sentences below have in common? Does the verb *were* seem to fit?

> If she <u>were</u> present, she'd vote against the issue.
>
> If it <u>were</u> possible, he'd undo the damage his recklessness caused.
>
> If I <u>were</u> you, I'd save some money for a rainy day.
>
> Fido acts as if he <u>were</u> human.

In the four sentences above, notice that *if* or *as if* introduces a condition that doesn't exist. In indicative sentences the verb would be *was* for the singular pronouns *she, it, I,* and *he.* In everyday speech you often hear indicative mood when standard English would be subjunctive mood.

The subjunctive mood expresses conditions not actually in existence: wishes, hypothetical situations, or statements contrary to fact.

Does that mean that all *if* clauses require *were*? No. When choosing between *was* and *were* in clauses beginning with *if,* decide if the sentence requires subjunctive mood—that is, if the clause involves nonexistent conditions.

Compare the sentences below.

> If I <u>was</u> rude, I apologize.
>
> If I <u>were</u> as rude as Rudy, I wouldn't have any friends.

Notice that the first sentence above indicates a situation that might have actually existed; the second sentence is merely hypothetical. Only the second sentence uses subjunctive mood.

Compare the sentences below.

> If it <u>was</u> my aunt who called, she'll call again.
>
> If it <u>were</u> my aunt instead of my uncle who called, we'd still be on the phone.

Notice that the first sentence above merely indicates a lack of knowledge, not a hypothetical situation as in the second sentence. A lack of knowledge does not require subjunctive mood. The second sentence, however, is hypothetical and uses subjunctive mood.

A non-existing condition may also begin with *unless,* as in the sentence below.

> Unless the sun <u>were</u> to rise in the west, I wouldn't count on a veto.

The sentences below also use *were* with a singular pronoun or noun for the subjunctive mood but aren't introduced by *if, as if,* or *unless.* What do they have in common?

> I wish I <u>were</u> in Hawaii right now.
>
> Everyone wishes Hector <u>were</u> still with us.

Each sentence above discusses a wish, another condition that doesn't exist.

Besides *were,* subjunctive mood takes other verb forms. Examine the use of *be* in the sentences below. What do the sentences have in common?

> He suggested *that* they just <u>be</u> friends.
>
> It is important *that* he <u>be</u> discreet in this matter.
>
> The new guidelines require *that* budgets <u>be</u> submitted by September.

Notice that all three sentences above use *be* to express wishes, which may take the form of demands, requests, or requirements. It doesn't matter if the subject is plural (*they* or *budgets*) or singular (*he*). Did you notice that each subjunctive mood clause begins with *that*?

Notice how other verbs express demands or requests in other *that* clauses in the following sentences.

His lawyer asked *that* he <u>bring</u> the documents.

Her parents demanded *that* she not <u>speak</u> unless spoken to.

The legislature's request *that* the governor <u>recognize</u> its mandate was ignored.

The coach insists *that* each player <u>complete</u> his assignments before practice.

Our new counselor recommends *that* every student <u>schedule</u> an interview.

The airlines' requirement *that* each passenger <u>arrive</u> early was not well received.

The sentences above express demands or requests (subjunctive mood because they are nonexistent conditions) by using what would normally be a plural verb form (without a helping verb) for third person. That is, in a non-subjunctive situation, the verbs *brings, speaks, completes, recognizes, schedules,* and *arrives* would be used with the singular subjects *he, she, governor, player, student,* and *passenger.*

Subjunctive mood is common in several traditional expressions:

If need <u>be</u>, we can hold a special election.

If that's what they want, so <u>be</u> it.

Far <u>be</u> it from me to question his authority.

<u>Be</u> that as it may, you still must complete the assignment.

The book, as it <u>were</u>, sold a million copies, even after the negative publicity.

We will work things out, <u>come</u> what may.

Long <u>live</u> the queen.

If it <u>be</u> your will, I will obey.

As you can see, there is no consistent pattern with the idiomatic (common) expressions above. Some don't even fit the usual pattern or purposes of subjunctive moods, yet they are accepted uses of the subjunctive mood.

Avoid Shifts in Mood

Compare the two sentences below and speculate why the second is preferable.

I suggested that she <u>keep</u> a journal and <u>uses</u> it for story ideas.

I suggested that she <u>keep</u> a journal and <u>use</u> it for story ideas.

The first sentence above shifts moods from subjunctive to indicative. The second sentence maintains subjunctive mood. **Avoid shifts of mood.**

Mood shifts may involve any moods. Examine the following mood shifts and revisions.

Original—<u>Signal</u> before turning and <u>you should make</u> your intentions clear.

Revision #1—<u>Signal</u> before turning and <u>make</u> your intentions clear.

    or

Revision #2—<u>You should signal</u> before turning and <u>make</u> your intentions clear.

Original—If I <u>were</u> promoted and he <u>was</u> passed over, he'd probably resign.

Revised—If I <u>were</u> promoted and he <u>were</u> passed over, he'd probably resign.

In the first sentence above, the shift from imperative mood to indicative is revised by making both halves of the sentence imperative or by making both indicative (with *should* as a helping verb for both *signal* and *make*). In the second sentence, the shift from subjunctive to indicative is revised by making both verbs subjunctive.

Practice

In the sentences below, change verbs where appropriate to form the standard subjunctive mood. Some sentences may already have the standard verb form.

1. If Brett was to apply himself, he could be an excellent writer.
2. Her main concern was that her son be honest.
3. Ava decided that if he was late for the date, she would go with someone else.
4. If he were stranded on a moon made of cheese, it would be just desserts for the dirty rat.
5. Unless he was to have a sudden shift in personality, I wouldn't expect sensitivity.
6. His mother insists that he flosses every day.
7. The instructions suggest that the operator maintain a service record and keeps it current.
8. Nature demands that every creature eventually dies.

Adverbs

Recalling the five functions of words (naming, describing, showing action or being, connecting), determine what the underlined words do in the sentences below.

> Walter <u>quickly</u> admits his mistakes.
> He <u>always</u> sends his wife a gift when he's on the road.
> We lived <u>there</u> for three years.

If you said the underlined words describe, you are right. What kind of words do they describe? What do they tell or what questions do they answer about the words they describe?

All three underlined words above describe verbs *(admits, sends,* and *lived)* and tell <u>how</u>, <u>when</u>, and <u>where</u>.

In the sentences below, what words do the underlined words describe, and what questions do they answer?

> I was surprised to see a frown on her <u>usually</u> happy face.
> Her new car is <u>bright</u> red.
> This grade makes me <u>very</u> happy.

The underlined words describe adjectives (*happy, red* and *happy*) and tell <u>when</u>, <u>how</u>, and <u>to what degree.</u> **Words that describe verbs or adjectives are called adverbs. They tell how, when, where, why, and to what degree.**

Adverbs can do one more thing. In the sentences below, what do the underlined adverbs describe?

> He changed the subject <u>rather</u> quickly.
> The subject was <u>somewhat</u> delicately discussed.

In the first sentence above, *rather* describes *quickly*, another adverb which describes the verb *changed.* In the second sentence, *somewhat* describes *delicately,* another adverb which describes the verb *discussed.* Thus, besides describing verbs and adjectives, **adverbs can describe other adverbs.**

This may seem a bit confusing at first, but it will get easier as you become more familiar with relationships among words. Find the adverbs in the following sentences.

> Our trip was very loosely planned.
> The test was not very hard.

In the first sentence above, the adverb *very* describes *loosely*, an adverb that describes the verb *planned*. In the second sentence the adverb *not* describes *very*, an adverb that describes the adjective *hard*. Incidentally, what are the adverbs if the sentence is rewritten as below?

> The test wasn't very hard.

The *was* part of *wasn't* is a verb, and the *-n't* part is a contracted adverb, *not*, describing the adverb *very*. We frequently use apostrophes in contractions to connect verbs and adverbs: *couldn't, hasn't, can't, aren't, shouldn't, isn't, wouldn't, don't, won't.* Notice that *won't* contracts *will not*, an interesting variation.

Notice the location of the adverbs in relation to the words they describe in the sentences below. Is there a consistent pattern?

> <u>Somehow</u> we must find the answer.
> We ordered the books <u>Thursday</u>.
> You must <u>simply</u> sing from the heart.
> I saw him <u>only</u> yesterday.

Adverbs have many locations. *Somehow* describes *must find* but begins the sentence separate from the verb. *Thursday* describes *ordered* but ends the sentence separate from the verb. *Simply* describes *must sing* and comes between the two parts of the verb phrase. *Only* describes and immediately precedes *yesterday*. In some cases the adverb's location is important to avoid confusion, but in other cases the location is optional.

Practice

Find the adverbs in the following sentences. It may help initially to find verbs and adjectives first, then the adverbs that tell how, when, where, and to what degree.

1. He left yesterday.
2. I will leave here soon.
3. Our love will last forever.
4. She entered reluctantly.
5. He visited his seriously ill grandmother.
6. I was completely wrong.
7. We tentatively reached an agreement.
8. The race is just too long.
9. She hasn't called yet.
10. I put the money there.
11. She quickly retracted her somewhat hasty statement.
12. You may be thoroughly confused, if not absolutely baffled.

<u>Comparative and Superlative Adverbs</u>

Like adjectives, adverbs can be comparative and superlative. What patterns do you see with the adverbs in the sentences below?

> Lance responds <u>more quickly</u> than Morris.
> Lance responds <u>most quickly</u> with a deadline.
> She eats <u>slower</u> than I do.
> She eats <u>slowest</u> of all the students.

Adverbs use the same forms as adjectives for comparative and superlative degree. **Adverbs show comparative degree by adding *-er* or *more;* adverbs show superlative degree by adding *-est* or *most.***

Practice
In the sentences below, correct any nonstandard comparative or superlative forms of adjectives and adverbs. Some may be correct already.
1. That was the strangest book I've read.
2. Of the two, Drew's car ran more efficiently.
3. She critiqued my second paper carefuller than the first.
4. Hers were the most positive criticisms I received.
5. My brother can look sadder than a bloodhound.
6. Between my parents, my mother is most perceptive.
7. Of the two planets, Jupiter is the larger.
8. Avery is gracefuler than her sister.

Conjunctions

Recalling the five functions of words (naming, describing, showing action or being, connecting), determine what the underlined words do in the sentences below.

Dolphins <u>and</u> whales are mammals.
We are expecting a call tomorrow at eight <u>or</u> nine.

If you said they connect, you are right. In the sentences above, *and* and *or* connect individual words. What do they connect in the following sentences?

Dow-Jones averages are up, <u>and</u> the economy looks brighter.
You will find the money in the drawer <u>or</u> on the cabinet.

Notice that these words can connect ideas or groups of words: In the first sentence, *and* connects "Dow-Jones averages are up" to "the economy looks brighter." In the second sentence, *or* connects "in the drawer" to "on the cabinet." **Words like these that connect words, phrases, or clauses are called <u>conjunctions.</u>**

Many conjunctions indicate a particular kind of relationship between the things they connect. What might be the relationship between the two sentences below? Could you express that relationship with a conjunction?
She left the meeting. She felt ill.

The second sentence might be the cause of the first. Below are two possible causal connections.
She left the meeting <u>because</u> she felt ill.
She felt ill, <u>so</u> she left the meeting.

The conjunctions *because* and *so* show a cause-and-effect relationship.
What relationships are expressed by the conjunctions in the sentences below?
We left a tip, <u>but</u> it wasn't enough.
You will fail the test <u>unless</u> you study.
I'll call you <u>when</u> I get some news.

But shows a contrast relationship, *unless* shows a conditional relationship, and *when* shows a time relationship.

All the conjunctions above come between the things they connect. Is that the only location for conjunctions? Can you rearrange the following sentences to put the conjunction first?

> You can keep the kitten <u>if</u> you'll give it a good home.
> My perspective has really changed <u>since</u> I've been in college.

Yes, some conjunctions can be located at the beginning or in the middle of a sentence, so you could rearrange the sentences above to read:

> If you'll give it a good home, you can keep the kitten.
> Since I've been in college, my perspective has really changed.

Find the conjunctions in the below. Tell what they connect and what relationship they show. (For example, in the sentence, "He lives carefully but happily," the conjunction *but* connects *carefully* and *happily,* showing contrast.)

> After the concert ended, Madonna signed autographs.
> It stopped raining, so we resumed our ride.
> You can pay me now or pay me later.
> As a duck takes to water, he took to politics.
> It will be a cold day in the Baja before I talk with her again.
> Although electricity is cleaner, gas is less expensive.
> You improved greatly because you practiced.

After (time) connects "the concert ended" to "Madonna signed autographs.
So (cause and effect) connects "It stopped raining" to "we resumed our ride."
Or (contrast) connects "pay me now" to "pay me later."
As (similarity) connects "a duck takes to water" with "he took to politics."
Before (time) connects "It will be a cold day in the Baja" with "I talk with her again."
Although (contrast) connects "electricity is cleaner" with "gas is less expensive."
Because (cause and effect) connects "You improved greatly" to "you practiced."

Conjunctions are divided into three types, <u>coordinating</u>, <u>subordinating</u>, and <u>correlative</u>. We will now examine them separately.

Coordinating Conjunctions
Coordinating conjunctions are *and, or, but, nor, for, so* and *yet.*

In the sentences below find the coordinating conjunctions, noticing what they connect and where they are located.

> She has three dogs and a cat.
> The instructions seemed clear, yet few people followed them correctly.
> Mr. Smith said John or Sam will call you.
> We will keep you informed, for you have a right to know.
> We have plenty of ideas but limited resources.

And connects "three dogs" with "a cat."
Yet connects "The instructions seemed clear" with "few people followed them correctly."
Or connects "John" with "Sam."
For connects "We will keep you informed" with "you have a right to know."
But connects "plenty of ideas" with "limited resources."

Coordinating conjunctions always come between the things they connect. They can connect single words or groups of words. Things connected by coordinating conjunctions are considered equal (thus, the prefix co- in coordinating).

Subordinating Conjunctions

Subordinating conjunctions are listed below. A subordinating conjunction may be more than one word.

after	although	as	as if	as though
because	before	even if	even though	how
if	in case	in order that	in order to	inasmuch as
insofar as	in that	lest	no matter how	now that
once	provided	provided that	since	so that
supposing	than	that	though	till
unless	until	when	whenever	where
whereas	wherever	whether	while	why

The subordinating conjunction maks the idea it introduces dependent on (subordinate to) the main idea of the sentence. In the following sentence, for example, the main idea is the first one:

<u>I don't care for licorice</u> although I liked it as a child.
        main idea   subordinate idea

The subordinating conjunction *although* connects the two ideas, showing contrast.

In the following sentences, find the main idea and the subordinated idea.

<u>Since</u> we found the puppy, he has grown a foot taller.

We will have to find another manager <u>when</u> Jim retires.

I will write every day <u>until</u> I see you again.

<u>If</u> no one objects, we can take the afternoon off.

We had three applications <u>after</u> the deadline passed.

<u>Whenever</u> Jack talks, he uses a lot of facial expression.

Correlative Conjunctions

Correlative conjunctions come in two parts: *either/or, neither/nor, both/and, whether/or, not only/but also*. See the examples below:

1. <u>Whether</u> you like it <u>or</u> not, nuclear power is probably here to stay.
2. <u>Neither</u> the dean <u>nor</u> the chairman knows of her withdrawal.
3. You may select <u>either</u> a freshman <u>or</u> a sophomore.
4. She is <u>both</u> articulate <u>and</u> assertive.
5. The report is <u>not only</u> late <u>but also</u> incomplete.

Why use correlative conjunctions? Often they indicate choices (*either/or, neither/nor, whether/or*), but they have another common use. Compare sentences #4 and #5 above to the two sentences below. Why might you choose the correlative conjunctions above instead of just using *and* as below?

She is articulate and assertive.

The report is late and incomplete.

The correlative conjunctions *both/and* and *not only/but also* are often used for emphasis. Find the correlative conjunctions in the following sentences.

I can't decide whether to go bicycling or to take a nap.

Both the United States and the Soviet Union continue to increase armaments.

It is neither convenient nor economical to change systems now.

Not only did he win the competition, but he also set a record.

Either David or Randy could receive the award.

The correlative conjunctions in the sentences above are *whether/or, both/and, neither/nor, not only/but also,* and *either/or.*

Practice

Find all three types of conjunctions in the sentences below.

1. Lyle and Michael stayed until the snow melted.
2. Unless you rake every week, leaves can take over your yard.
3. Her mom waited patiently as Jill listened to the end of the song.
4. Neither the hamsters nor the cat will go hungry while you're gone.
5. Please give me some time, or I can't possibly make the payment.
6. You can't go outside until you finish your homework.
7. The stranger seemed nice yet mysterious.
8. If you can find them, please return my hammer, saw, and screwdriver.
9. Carl ordered the CD because he read a good review.
10. Jan is not only a superb swimmer but also a champion fencer.

Prepositions

Analyze the underlined phrases in the sentences below and answer three questions: What does each phrase tell about the rest of the sentence? With what kind of word does each phrase end? What word in the phrase connects the last word to the rest of the sentence?

The bird flew <u>through the window.</u>

Their house is <u>by the river.</u>

She stood <u>beside him.</u>

The above phrases all tell *where*. Each phrase ends with a noun or pronoun, which is connected to the rest of the sentence by the first word in the phrase. The first word of each of these phrases is called a **preposition.** Without the preposition, the noun would be left hanging. Without the noun, the preposition would be left hanging. For example, we normally wouldn't think of *him* as a location, and *beside* alone doesn't give the location, but the whole phrase does.

A group of words beginning with a preposition and ending with a noun or pronoun is called a <u>prepositional phrase</u>. The noun or pronoun at the end of the prepositional phrase is called the <u>object of the preposition</u>.

Since the prepositional phrases above tell *where*, they act as adverbs.

What do the prepositional phrases below show?

He sleeps <u>during most classes.</u>

I'd never met her <u>until last week.</u>

<u>In the morning</u> a rooster awakened me.

The phrases above show *when*, the second most common use of prepositional phrases. What word does "during most classes" describe? It describes *sleeps*. Because *sleeps* is a verb, how is the prepositional phrase "during most classes" used (what part of speech)? It is used as an adverb, as are the phrases "until last week" (to describe *met)* and "in the morning" (to describe *awakened).*

In the sentences below, what word does each prepositional phrase describe?

> The bird <u>on the windowsill</u> has been chirping all morning.
> Her favorite book <u>by Emile Zola</u> is *The Paradise*.
> His birthday is the day <u>before Christmas</u>.

"On the windowsill" describes "bird"; "by Emile Zola" describes "book"; "before Christmas" describes "day." What kind of words are *bird, book,* and *day*?

Bird, book, and *day* are nouns, so those three prepositional phrases are used as adjectives, telling *which one,* (one of the three adjective questions – which one, what kind, how many?)
You might be thinking that "on the windowsill" and "before Christmas" also answer adverb questions *where* and *when* – which they do, but since the phrases describe nouns, they're considered adjectives.

Prepositional phrases are always used as adjectives or adverbs to describe.

By determining what it describes, decide whether each prepositional phrase below is an adjective or adverb.

> <u>Like her mother</u> she loves to read.
> The painting is a copy <u>of a Van Gogh</u>.
> They went sailing <u>despite the storm warnings</u>.
> The newspaper related the story <u>about the accident</u>.
> We traveled <u>along the coast</u> for a week.

"Like her mother" (adjective) describes *she*; "of a Van Gogh" (adjective) describes *copy*; "despite the storm warnings" (adverb) describes *went*; "about the accident" (adjective) describes *story*; "along the coast" (adverb) describes *traveled*.

Below is a list of common prepositions:

about	above	across	after	against
along	among	around	as	at
before	behind	below	beneath	beside
besides	between	beyond	but	by
concerning	despite	down	during	except
for	from	in	inside	into
like	near	of	off	on
onto	out	outside	over	past
regarding	since	through	throughout	to
toward	under	underneath	unlike	until
up	upon	with	within	without

Instead of trying to memorize prepositions, learn them by noticing them in your own writing and in your reading. Concentrate on those you don't immediately recognize as prepositions. The most commonly unrecognized prepositions are *like* and *but,* perhaps because they are also used as other parts of speech. Compare their use below:

> His face was narrow <u>like</u> a hatchet.
> I <u>like</u> chocolate truffles.

> Everyone <u>but</u> Lisa will be there.
> The glass was cracked, <u>but</u> no one noticed.

"Like a hatchet" is a prepositional phrase, while *like* in the second sentence is a verb.
"But Lisa" is a prepositional phrase (you could substitute *except*); *but* in the second sentence is a conjunction connecting two ideas.

Several prepositions *(after, as, before, for, since, until)* can also be used as conjunctions. How can you tell the difference? Analyze their relationship with other words in the sentence.

Decide if the underlined words below are prepositions or conjunctions.
>   We found mud in every room of the house *after* the flood.
>   We found mud in every room of the house *after* the flood ended.

In the first sentence above, "after the flood" is a prepositional phrase; in the second sentence, "the flood ended" is an idea connected by the conjunction *after* to the rest of the sentence.

Compare the pairs of sentences below to determine prepositions and conjunctions.
>   a. The finish was smooth <u>as</u> silk.
>   b. <u>As</u> we left, the roof collapsed.
>   c. <u>Before</u> you leave, please give me the number.
>   d. <u>Before</u> the banquet the speaker lost his voice.
>   e. Amos looked everywhere <u>for</u> the ring.
>   f. She was convinced she would win, <u>for</u> she had trained furious.
>   g. <u>Since</u> the collapse of the Roman Empire, all roads do not lead to Rome.
>   h. <u>Since</u> you insist on playing the fool, here is your jester's cap.
>   i. The bank will not approve the loan <u>until</u> you provide collateral.
>   j. <u>Until</u> the next show we can wait in the lobby.

The underlined words in the sentence pairs above are used as follows: a. preposition, b. conjunction; c. conjunction, d. preposition; e. preposition, f. conjunction; g. preposition, h. conjunction; i. conjunction, j. preposition.

Practice
Find prepositional phrases, pointing out the prepositions and their objects in the sentences below:
1. To my knowledge no one failed the test.
2. We looked for hours for the tiny screw.
3. The rocker under the elm is Grandpa's favorite spot.
4. Take your application to the business office.
5. He gave a negative review on the movie about the Civil War.
6. Without a doubt, it was a great performance.
7. Anyone with a problem should see her advisor about it.
8. The letter from the mayor urged immediate action on the project.
9. The noise outside the classroom disrupted the reading of *Macbeth*.
10. On the table in the middle of the room is a magnificent vase.

Conjunctive Adverbs

Recalling the five functions of words (naming, describing, showing action or being, connecting) determine what the underlined words do in the sentences below.

> She failed the first semester; <u>likewise</u>, her father had failed his first year.
> Leave the car in the garage; <u>otherwise</u>, you'll get into trouble.
> I spent ten hours studying; <u>therefore</u>, I expect to make a good grade.
> It rained for three hours in Kingston; <u>meanwhile</u>, it was snowing in Guymon.

The underlined words connect and show relationships of similarity, contrast, cause and effect, and time. You might initially want to call them conjunctions, but which of the three types of conjunctions would they be—coordinating, subordinating, or correlative?

They are single words, so that rules out correlative (always two parts such as *neither/nor*).
They are not on the list of coordinating conjunctions: *and, or, but, nor, for, yet, so.*
If they were subordinating conjunctions, you could flip the ideas and begin with the underlined word: "Otherwise, you'll get into trouble, leave the car in the garage." As you can see, that doesn't work. Furthermore, (unlike sentences with subordinating conjunctions) the last half of the sentence beginning with the underlined word can stand alone, e.g., "Meanwhile, it was snowing in Guymon."

These connecting words are not conjunctions, but conjunctive adverbs. **Conjunctive adverbs are adverbs used to connect ideas and show relationships.**

Notice also the special punctuation of the conjunctive adverb:

> I plan to get up early tomorrow**;** otherwise, I'll miss my bus.

When it comes between two ideas in a single sentence, a conjunctive adverb is preceded by a semicolon and followed by a comma.

What if the conjunctive adverb begins a new sentence or interrupts a single idea?

> I plan to get up early tomorrow. <u>Otherwise</u>, I'll miss my bus.
> It is getting late. I think, <u>therefore</u>, we should leave.

If a conjunctive adverb begins a sentence, it is followed by a comma. If it interrupts a single idea, a conjunctive adverb is usually separated by commas. To help internalize the patterns of conjunctive adverbs and punctuation, see the sentences below.
1. Sarah is on vacation; however, she will return Friday.
2. The renters missed six payments; therefore, they were evicted.
3. In 1986 we made a profit; likewise, we expect a profit this year.
4. We'd like a nice raise. We will, however, settle for shorter hours.
5. The parade starts at six. You should, therefore, be in place by 5:30.
6. His history grade went up. Likewise, his algebra grade improved.

Below is a list of conjunctive adverbs:

accordingly	additionally	also	anyway	besides
certainly	consequently	conversely	finally	furthermore
hence	however	incidentally	indeed	instead

likewise	meanwhile	moreover	nevertheless	next
nonetheless	now	otherwise	similarly	still
subsequently	then	thereafter	therefore	thus
undoubtedly				

Transitional Phrases

Transitional phrases are similar to conjunctive adverbs, used to make connections and punctuated like conjunctive adverbs. Below is a list of common transitional phrases:

after all	as a matter of fact	as a result	at any rate
at the same time	by the same token	even so	for example
for instance	in addition	in conclusion	in context
in fact	in like manner	in other words	in similar fashion
in the first place	in the same way	on the contrary	on the other hand

Practice

Find the conjunctive adverbs and transitional phrases in the following sentences:

1. Give me a little more time; undoubtedly, two hours will suffice.
2. He missed three payments; as a result, they repossessed his car.
3. We searched for hours; finally, we found the ring in the garden.
4. Tim worked on his own; in like manner, Rob finished his job alone.
5. I quit. Furthermore, my friends quit.
6. Tracie missed the tryout; she was, nevertheless, selected for the group.
7. His arguments are weak; still, he has quite a following.
8. Dr. Wallaby is a great philanthropist. Accordingly, he was honored.

Interjections

The last Part of Speech is the interjection. Below are examples.

<u>Wow</u>! This is the last one?

<u>Yes</u>, it is.

<u>Hmm</u>, really?

<u>Well</u>, that's a relief.

<u>Okay</u>, we'll eventually define interjections.

Fortunately, a few examples like this should give you the idea of the dozens of interjections. Actually, there's no definite list of interjections because they may be made-up words.

<u>Golly Gee Willikers</u>!

Here are more examples of interjections.

No way!

Hello.

Goodbye.

Please, answer the question.

Congratulations.

Hey, watch where you're going.

Stop!

Interjections are words or phrases used to show strong feeling or emotion, to answer questions, to indicate pauses, to give commands, to show approval, and to get attention. They may be separated from sentences with periods, question marks, or explanation points. If in a sentence, they are usually separated with commas and have no grammatical relationship to the rest of the sentence.

Parts of Speech P.S.

The word functions we have been discussing – nouns, pronouns, adjectives, verbs, adverbs, conjunctions, prepositions, and interjections – are called <u>parts of speech</u>.

<u>Remember: grammar terminology is not our focus,</u> but terminology can help us as we analyze sentences and learn the concepts of grammar. If you have analyzed and learned each concept carefully, you are well on your way to a genuine understanding of grammar and usage.

One word of caution: Many words can be used in more than one way. Analyze the different uses of *pioneer* in the following sentences:

> Oklahomans take pride in their <u>pioneer</u> spirit.
> My great grandmother was a <u>pioneer</u> who came west.
> Someday this company will <u>pioneer</u> new technology.

Pioneer is used as an adjective in the first sentence, a noun in the second sentence, and a verb in the third.

Analyze the use of *after* in the following sentences:

> We went home <u>after</u> the movie.
> <u>After</u> the President spoke, the networks interpreted his message.
> Jack fell down and broke his crown, and Jill came tumbling <u>after</u>.

After is used above as a preposition in the first sentence, a conjunction in the second, and an adverb in the third.

Because words have many uses, you cannot simply memorize lists of prepositions, conjunctions, etc. and hope to do well in grammar. Instead, you must do what we have been doing since the beginning of these lessons: Analyze the relationships among the words and recognize patterns.

Practice

To reinforce your understanding of the concepts and your ability to analyze, try to identify all the parts of speech in the following sentences:

1. The car ran into the telephone pole.
2. Everyone in the group had enough money for a room.
3. Money can't buy love.
4. This is a horse of a different color.
5. He set a record in the triathlon.
6. He found himself between a rock and a hard place.
7. Because she had the best record, she was given a promotion.
8. Yes, computer can increase productivity greatly.
9. She spoke softly, but we got the idea.
10. That concludes the lesson unless someone has a question.

Five Basic Sentence Patterns: From the beginning of this book, we have talked about patterns. For example, prepositional phrases are patterns: a preposition followed by a noun or pronoun, sometimes with descriptive words between the preposition and the noun or pronoun. Whole sentences have patterns that we will now explore, beginning with the most basic.

Pattern One – Predicate Adjectives

What is the following sentence about?
> Grammar is important.

Since the sentence is about *grammar,* we say that *grammar* is the <u>subject</u> of the sentence.

The term <u>subject</u> is used for what a sentence is about.

What part of speech (adjective, noun, verb, etc.) is *grammar*?
What parts of speech are the other two words in the sentence?
What does *important* do in the sentence?

If you said *grammar* is a noun, *is* is a verb, and *important* is an adjective describing *grammar,* you are right. **This is one of the basic patterns of a sentence: a subject with a <u>being</u> verb that links the subject to an adjective describing the subject.** (Remember from the earlier discussion of verbs that <u>being</u> verbs are words like *is, are, was, were, could be, has been, might have been,* etc.)

Most adjectives come before the words they describe (e.g., the <u>tall</u>, <u>skinny</u> player). But because the purpose of a pattern one sentence is to describe, the adjective is separated from the subject and placed at the end for emphasis. Notice that pattern below:
> The dog was huge.
> Her performance was magnificent.
> Roosevelt was popular.

The verb along with other words after it is called a <u>complete predicate</u>. The verb by itself is called a <u>simple predicate</u>. In sentence pattern one, an adjective in the complete predicate describes the subject and is called a <u>predicate adjective</u>. Predicate adjectives are sometimes called "subject complements" because they complete (complement) the subject. (*Complement* is different from *compliment.*)

Find the predicate adjectives in the following sentences. What do you notice about the verbs?
> That fabric feels rough.
> His voice sounds harsh and raspy.
> This stew tastes delicious.
> The trunk smelled somewhat musty.
> He really looks handsome in his new suit.

The predicate adjectives above are *rough, harsh* and *raspy, delicious, musty,* and *handsome.* Did you notice that these verbs are not <u>being verbs</u>? What do the verbs *feels, sounds, tastes, smelled,* and *looks* have in common? They involve the five senses, and in the sentences above they connect subjects to predicate adjectives, and are called <u>sense verbs</u>.

What about the verbs below? Do they connect subjects and predicate adjectives?

> She appeared anxious about her recital.
> He grew restless waiting for the interview.
> They seem apprehensive about the test.
> His face turned red with embarrassment.

Yes, *appeared, grew, seem,* and *turned* connect subjects and predicate adjectives in these sentences.

Verbs for the five senses (as well as verbs like *appear, become, grow, get, remain, seem, stay,* and *turn*) often link subjects to predicate adjectives. Together with the being verbs they are called <u>linking</u> verbs when they connect adjectives to subjects.

Practice
Find all the predicate adjectives in the following sentences and notice the linking verbs. There may be more than one predicate adjective in some of the sentences.
1. I hope you're not too ambitious.
2. The leaves have turned red after the first frost, and it's getting cold.
3. She felt ill after eating the soup.
4. He said that the next workout will be rigorous.
5. As finals approach, she is getting anxious.
6. Sailors should stay alert even if the water becomes calm.
7. Be sure you keep calm when the discussion is tense.

Predicate adjectives are one of two types of <u>subject complements</u>, meaning that they complete the subject. (Notice *complements* differs from *compliments,* and has a different meaning. *Complement* means "completing.")

Pattern Two – Predicate Nominatives

What is the difference between the above sentences (pattern one) and those below?

> His sister is a cheerleader.
> My first class is English.

Like the pattern one sentences, each of the sentences above has a subject linked by a being verb to something in the predicate. But what part of speech are *cheerleader* and *English*?

They are nouns, and nouns name. In these sentences they rename the subject. Sometimes they're called <u>predicate nouns</u>, but since pronouns in the predicate can also rename subjects, a better term is <u>predicate nominatives</u> (*nominative* basically meaning *name*). **This is a second basic sentence pattern: a subject linked by a verb to a noun or pronoun (predicate nominative) renames the subject.** The predicate nominative is another subject complement (like the predicate adjective, referring to the subject.)

Identify the subjects and predicate nominatives below:

That school is a football factory.

In a few years he may be the president.

The man on the flagpole was an escape artist.

He became chairman after only three years.

The predicate nominatives above are *factory, president, artist,* and *chairman.*

Practice

Identify predicate adjectives and predicate nominatives in the sentences below.

1. The captain of the ship was a hero in the collision with the reef.
2. She looks so academic in her cap and gown.
3. She will surely be the new senator.
4. My uncle was incredibly frugal.
5. Without a doubt, spring is my favorite season.
6. He appears uncertain of his next move.
7. The bank's biggest attraction has been its interest rates.

Pattern Three – Direct Objects

Analyze the sentences below, comparing them to the sentence patterns in the preceding exercise.

He smashed the ball.

They selected a senior.

She really hit him.

I believe you.

Like pattern two sentences, each of the sentences above has a subject, followed by a verb, followed by a noun, but are the verbs action or linking? Do the nouns after the verbs rename the subject?

The verbs *smashed, selected, hit,* and *believe* are actions, unlike the verbs in pattern two sentences. Instead of renaming the subjects, the nouns *ball* and *senior* and the pronouns *him* and *you* receive the actions performed by the subjects. These receivers of action are called direct objects. **This is a third basic sentence pattern: a subject performs some action upon a direct object (noun or pronoun).** The direct object completes (complements) the verb. Remember that actions aren't always physical (e.g., *selected* and *believe* above).

Practice

Find the direct objects below, selecting the nouns or pronouns receiving the action.

1. His dog pulled the leash out of Bill's hand.
2. After lunch we bought a pastry.
3. In the long run, carbohydrates surpass fats.
4. After a good start he rode his bike off the road.
5. In the old westerns, the good guys always wore white hats.
6. Mike Powell surpassed Bob Beamon's record for the long jump.
7. We discovered the discrepancy just in time.
8. Ultimately, you must accept responsibility for your actions.

Pattern Four – Indirect Objects

What is the difference between the first and second sentence in each pair below?

      1a. She gave five dollars.
      1b. She gave me five dollars.
      2a. He threw a curve.
      2b. He threw me a curve.

The first and third sentences are pattern three with subject, verb, and direct object, but the second and fourth sentences interrupt that pattern with "me." The sentences could have been written, "She gave five dollars to me" and "He threw a curve to me," including "me" in prepositional phrases. We often use the pattern of sentences 1b and 2b above to indicate <u>to whom</u> or <u>for whom</u>, <u>to what</u> or <u>for what</u> something is done to something else - omitting the *to* or *for*. **A word that tells <u>to whom/what</u> or <u>for whom/what</u> an action is done is called an <u>indirect object.</u>**

This is a fourth basic sentence pattern: a subject followed by an action verb, then an indirect object and a direct object. The indirect object always comes before a direct object.

Practice

Find the indirect objects and direct objects in the sentences below:

1. David sent his mother a postcard from Munich.
2. The last movement of Beethoven's Ninth gives me chills.
3. The professor offered his students two options for their final.
4. He bet me ten dollars on the game.
5. The real estate agent showed them a dozen homes.
6. Money will not buy you happiness.

Practice

Now see if you can identify predicate adjectives, predicate nominatives, direct objects, and indirect objects. The key is the relationship between the verb and what completes it. Does the verb act on a direct object and maybe an indirect object, or does the verb link the subject to a predicate adjective or predicate nominative?

1. My boss hosted a big party.
2. The business school is famous for its management program.
3. In the meantime, he will send you a memo with details.
4. My little brother says the dumbest things.
5. No one could possibly take your place.
6. Mr. Smothers is the new chairman of the board.
7. Their children seem bright and inquisitive.
8. Something in here smells rotten.
9. John gave Susan the key to the building.
10. The airline pilots seemed upset by the new regulations.
11. It was the most interesting book on the shelf.
12. Napoleon built his empire with force.
13. Sometimes I don't want anything but quiet.
14. Influenza can be contagious in all stages.
15. They had a strange but wonderful relationship.

Pattern Five

Now that you recognize patterns one, two, three, and four, see if the following sentences fit the pattern. Do they have predicate adjectives, predicate nominatives, direct objects or indirect objects?

> 1. He left without a good-bye.
> 2. The discussion lasted for three hours.
> 3. The baby cries incessantly.
> 4. She is always in a hurry.

No, they do not. Nothing renames the subject, no adjectives describe the subject, and no nouns or pronouns receive action from verbs.

Are actions always performed on something or someone (an object)? Sentences #1 and #2 begin with a subject and action verb, but instead of a direct object (something receiving the action) they are followed by prepositional phrases. In sentence #3 the action verb is followed only by an adverb, and in sentence #4 the linking verb is followed by an adverb and a prepositional phrase.

Many sentences with action verbs have no direct objects, and linking verbs may lack predicate adjectives or predicate nominatives. **A fifth basic sentence pattern is a subject and verb with no predicate adjective or predicate nominative or direct object or indirect object** (so no complements).

Practice

See if you can tell the difference between the sentence patterns below, labeling them pattern one (s-v-pa), two (s-v-pn), three (s-v-do), four (s-v-io-do), or five (s-v). Be careful not to confuse parts of prepositional phrases with direct objects, etc. For example, in the sentence "She peeked through the curtains," *curtains* is the object of the preposition *through,* not a direct object of *peeked.*

1. That guy is always looking for trouble.
2. Someone sent a bouquet of roses for her birthday.
3. The quarterback appears healthy again.
4. It is the same old story.
5. Sharon lived in Kansas for six years.
6. The race began with a false start.
7. I can never find two matching socks.
8. We looked diligently for the paper in every corner of the house.
9. Apathy is an unfortunate characteristic of some students.
10. The waves on the shore sound so soothing.

Variations of Basic Sentence Patterns

Of course, sentences don't all follow a straight subject-verb-complement (or no complement) pattern. The variations can make sentence analysis difficult. Examining common variations can be helpful.

<u>Commands</u>

Can you find subjects in the sentences below?

> Shut the door.
> Please remove your hat.
> Show me the best route to Nashville.

The sentences above lack subjects. **In these sentences, which are called <u>commands</u> or <u>imperatives</u>, the subject is understood to be the person to whom the command is given, so we say the subject is <u>the understood *you*.</u>** So the understood subjects and verbs above would be <u>you shut</u>, <u>you remove</u> and <u>you show</u>.

What about the sentence below? Is *Walter* the subject?

> Walter, tell them about the trip.

Even if a command contains a name, the subject is still the <u>understood *you*</u>. **The person addressed in the command is called a <u>direct address</u>**; it is not the subject. Thus, *Walter* is a direct address, and the understood *you* is the subject.

Questions

Other factors sometimes complicate sentence analysis. Find the subjects and verbs in the questions below. Hint: Find the verb(s) first, remembering that verbs often have helping verbs.

> 1. When does the train for Boston leave?
> 2. Did the plumber fix the sink?
> 3. Are you ready to leave yet?
> 4. What do you want for Christmas?
> 5. What will you tell your professor about the paper?

The subjects and verbs are "train does leave," "plumber did fix," "you are," "you do want," and "you will tell." What do you notice about word order in the questions above?

In all five sentences the verb precedes the subject. Sentence #1 begins with an adverb, followed by a helping verb *does*, followed by the subject *train* and a prepositional phrase, and then the main verb *leave*. Sentence #2 begins with the helping verb *did*, followed by the subject *plumber*, then the main verb *fix*, and then the direct object *sink*. Sentence #3 begins with the verb *are*, followed by the subject *you*, followed by the predicate adjective *ready*, and an infinitive, *to* plus a verb *leave* (infinitives will be discussed in another section) and an adverb. Sentence #4 begins with the direct object *what*, followed by the helping verb *do*, then the subject *you*, then the main verb *want*, and then a prepositional phrase. Sentence #5 begins with a direct object *what*, followed by the helping verb *will*, then the subject *you*, then an indirect object *your professor*, and then a prepositional phrase.

Questions are often inverted; that is, a verb and other words may come before the subject. Just remember to look for sentence inversions in most questions.

Here and *There*

Find the subjects in the sentences below:

> There are several good reasons for wearing seat belts.
> Here is the report for the last quarter.

Because many sentences follow a subject-verb-complement pattern, you might have said *there* and *here* are subjects in the sentences above. However, these sentences are another form of inversion. ***There* and *here* are always adverbs – never subjects.** So in the sentences above, *reasons* and *report* are the subjects. Just remember to look elsewhere for the subject (usually after the verb) when a sentence starts with *there* or *here*.

Compounds

Below we will examine forms of compounds: two or more words, phrases, or clauses. These compounds affect punctuation, subject-verb agreement, and pronoun-antecedent agreement.

Compound Parts of Sentences

Find subjects, verbs, predicate adjectives, predicate nominatives, direct objects, and indirect objects in the sentences below:

1. He writes excellent short stories and poetry
2. Dale and his brother are very different but very close.
3. The car dealer gave Jack and Jill a good deal on the used car.
4. She is his mentor and benefactor.

Notice that sentence #1 above has two direct objects (*stories* and *poetry*). Sentence #2 has two subjects (*Dale* and *brother*) and two predicate adjectives (*different* and *close*). Sentence #3 has two indirect objects (*Jack* and *Jill*). Sentence #4 has two predicate nominatives (*mentor* and *benefactor*). **Two or more subjects are called compound subjects. There may also be compound predicate nominatives, compound predicate adjectives, compound direct objects, or compound indirect objects.**

You might have noticed that the compounds above were all connected by the coordinating conjunction *and.* Do you suppose other conjunctions might connect compound? Also, could a compound be more than two? Examine the sentences below.

> The best rehearsal day might be Thursday or Friday.
> Should I call Avery or Teryn?
> The trio was Tom, Dick, and Harry.

Compounds may be connected by *or* and may include more than two.

Practice

What kinds of compounds can you find in the following sentences?
1. This problem is complex and frustrating.
2. The new principal has established discipline and enthusiasm in the school.
3. Is he a fool or a genius?
4. The company gave my dad and his assistant a new assignment.

Compound Phrases

Would you suppose that groups of words could be compounds as well? Analyze the sentences below.

> My name was called <u>after hers</u> but <u>before his</u>.
> Rob <u>finished the project</u> and <u>started a new one</u>.

The first sentence above contains compound prepositional phrases, "after her*s*" and "before his." The second sentence contains compound predicates, *finished the project* and *started a new one,* with each predicate containing its own verb and direct object.

Practice

Find sentence parts (subjects, verbs, predicate adjectives, predicate nominatives, indirect objects, and direct objects) in the variety of sentence patterns below. Remember, a sentence may contain compounds.
1. Television can be beneficial or harmful.
2. Neither Mom nor Dad seems very old in that picture.
3. Have you known him very long?

4. His "happy medium" is neither happy nor medium.

5. There is little chance of recovery.

6. Sean left her his phone number and address.

7. Put the money in an envelope and mail it by Friday.

8. Is there a long line at the ticket office?

9. The new officers will likely be Smith and Jones.

10. Someone called him a bad name.

11. What hope of success do we have?

12. Show me the files on the Bradford case.

13. Here is the spot with all the fish.

14. Why did you lie on the witness stand?

15. Radio advertisements are pretty inexpensive but very effective.

16. Where can I find the table and chairs?

17. Look into my eyes and tell me the truth.

18. Isn't his story somewhat unbelievable?

The sentence parts are labeled below.

           s.   p.a.   p.a.
Television can be beneficial or harmful.

           s.   s.   p.a.
Neither Mom nor Dad seems very old in that picture.

           s.   d.o.
Have you known him very long?

           s.   p.a.   p.a.
His "happy medium" is neither happy nor medium.

                 s.
There is little chance of recovery.

    s.   i.o.   d.o.   d.o.
Sean left her his phone number and address.

    s.   d.o.   d.o.
[you] Put the money in an envelope and mail it by Friday.

           s.
Is there a long line at the ticket office?

           s.   p.n.   p.n.
The new officers will likely be Smith and Jones.

     s.   i.o.   d.o.
Someone called him a bad name.

    d.o.   s.
What hope of success do we have?

    s.   i.o.   d.o.
[you] Show me the files on the Bradford case.

        s.
Here is the spot with all the fish.

        s.
Why did you lie on the witness stand?

        s.   p.a.   p.a.
Radio advertisements are pretty inexpensive but very effective.

    s.   d.o.   d.o.

Where can I find the table and chairs?

     s.   i.o.   d.o.

[you] Look into my eyes and tell me the truth.

     s.   p.a.

Isn't his story somewhat unbelievable?

Your ability to analyze sentences and recognize relationships among the parts is the foundation upon which other concepts can be built. If you had any trouble identifying the sentence parts in the examples above, look back through the explanations of sentence patterns and variations.

Compound Sentences

A sentence, as we have seen, contains at least a subject and a verb and expresses an idea. How many ideas does the sentence below contain?

     The Republicans won the Presidency, but the Democrats won Congress.

With the word *but* the sentence joins two ideas, each with its own subject and verb. These ideas are called *clauses*. **A compound sentence contains two or more clauses, each of which might be a separate sentence. Because the clauses in a compound sentence could each stand alone as a sentence, we call them** **independent clauses**.

To understand this better, compare the sentences below. What kind of compounds do they contain?

     He mowed the lawn and trimmed the hedge.
     He and she mowed the lawn.
     He and she mowed the lawn and trimmed the hedge.
     He mowed the lawn, and she trimmed the hedge.

The first sentence above contains a single subject with a compound predicate – one subject doing two things. The second sentence contains a compound subject with a single verb – two subjects doing one thing. The third sentence contains a compound subject and a compound predicate – both subjects doing both things. The fourth is a compound sentence with two ideas – one subject doing one thing and the other subject doing another thing.

Note that of the four sentences, only the compound sentence contains two independent clauses – two ideas that could each stand alone.

Not all sentences containing more than one idea (clause) are called compound sentences – only those with certain connectors. What are the connectors in the sentences below?

    1. She laughed, but he cried.
    2. Someone should call an ambulance, or he will die.
    3. He won't do the job himself, nor will he pay someone else.
    4. The rooster crowed, and the farm came alive.
    5. You must love me, for I love you.
    6. She seems to understand, yet she doesn't respond.
    7. Finish the job quickly; the deadline is Friday.
    8. Dewey was heavily favored; however, Truman won the election.
    9. I have an idea: let's sell cookies to raise money.

The first six sentences above connect clauses with coordinating conjunctions–*but, or, nor, and, for,* and *yet.* The seventh sentence connects clauses with a semicolon. The eighth sentence connects them with a semicolon and a conjunctive adverb, *however.* The ninth connects them with a colon. The punctuation marks will be discussed in detail later, but for now remember that **compound sentences join clauses with coordinating conjunctions, semicolons, semicolons with conjunctive adverbs, or colons.**

Complex Sentences with Adjective Clauses

We have seen how phrases can be used as adjectives, nouns, and adverbs – that is, a whole phrase such as "in the window" or "looking out the window" can be used as an adjective to describe a noun such as "cat." Let's take that a step further. In the sentences below compare functions of the underlined groups of words.

> We spoke to the legislator <u>for our district.</u>
> We spoke to the legislator <u>who represents our district.</u>

Both groups of words describe *legislator,* so they are used as adjectives. The first group is a prepositional phrase. What about the second group? Analyze its parts.

Who is the subject, *represents* is the verb, and *district* is a direct object. As we have seen in compound sentences, a group of words with a subject and verb expressing an idea is called a clause. Therefore, "who represents our district" is a clause. Could that clause be a separate sentence as a statement (not as a question)?

No, that clause could not be a separate sentence as a statement. Notice that "We spoke to the legislator" is an independent clause, which could stand alone. **Clauses are called <u>dependent clauses</u> if they depend on an independent clause to make a complete sentence**. Dependent clauses have various functions in sentences.

As noted above, "who represents our district" is used as an adjective because it describes the noun *legislator* in the main clause. **A dependent clause used as an adjective is called an <u>adjective clause.</u>**

What do you notice about the placement of the adjective clause in the sentence below?

> The legislator <u>who represents our district</u> will speak at the dinner.

The adjective clause, "who represents our district," interrupts the independent clause, "The legislator will speak at the dinner." Such interruptions are common.

Find the adjective clauses in the following sentences, noticing the words that begin the adjective clauses and noticing what word each clause describes.

> She sent an invitation that smelled of perfume.
> The trolley, which had run for thirty years, was discontinued.
> The class elected David, whom we had earlier ridiculed.
> I have no idea what you mean.
> I remember a time when he wasn't so confident.
> I'm trying to find the house where I lived as a child.

The adjective clauses and the words they described are as follows: "that smelled of perfume" describes *invitation*; "which had run for thirty years" describes *trolley*; "whom we had earlier ridiculed" describes *David*; "what you mean" describes *idea*; "when he wasn't so confident" describes *time*; and "where I lived as a child" describes *house.* Each of the adjective clauses above describes a noun or pronoun in the independent clause.

As you can see, **adjective clauses usually begin with relative pronouns (*that, what, whatever, which, whichever, who, whom, whose, whoever,* and *whomever*) but sometimes begin with *what, when* or *where.***

When a sentence contains an independent clause and a dependent clause, we call it a **complex sentence**. The independent clause is also called the *main* clause, and the dependent clause is also called the *subordinate* clause. The prefix *sub-* meaning "below" indicates that the subordinate clause is less important than the main clause.

Complex Sentences with Adverb Clauses

Do you suppose complex sentences might contain other types of dependent clauses besides adjective clauses? Analyze the sentences below and decide what the underlined clauses tell about the main clauses.

> After the snowstorm passed, we built a twelve-foot snowman.
> You were chosen because you seem honest and sincere.
> Hunting is prohibited where signs are posted.
> He gripped the ball as though it were a piece of fruit.
> If we watch our spending, we can stay within our budget.

The dependent clauses above tell *when, why, where, how,* and *under what conditions.* What part of speech answers those questions?

Adverbs answer those questions, and **clauses that act as adverbs are adverb clauses.** Notice the words that introduce the clauses. You may recall from an earlier discussion that subordinating conjunctions show relationships (time, cause and effect, location, degree, and condition) between ideas.

Following is a list of commonly used subordinating conjunctions.

after	although	as	as if	as though
because	before	even if	even though	how
if	in case	in order that	in order to	inasmuch as
insofar as	in that	lest	no matter how	now that
once	provided	provided that	since	so that
supposing	than	that	though	till
unless	until	when	whenever	where
whereas	wherever	whether	while	why

Instead of trying to memorize these conjunctions, find them in the sentences below, noticing the adverb clauses they connect with independent clauses.

> Although Leah is studious, she is by no means unsociable.
> You will lose your license unless you renew it this month.
> In the fall we plan a trip to New Hampshire as the leaves turn.
> Until the story was printed in the newspaper, no one suspected him.
> She will feel more comfortable once the shares are sold.
> Before you make the call, make sure your facts are straight.

The adverb clauses above include "Although Leah is studious"; "unless you renew it this month"; "as the leaves turn"; "Until the story was printed in the newspaper"; "once the shares are sold"; and "Before you make the call."

Caution: Don't immediately assume that every word on the list of subordinating conjunctions introduces an adverb clause. As we have seen in an earlier discussion, words such as *until, after,* and *before* may be used as prepositions. Remember too that *when* and *where* may introduce <u>adjective</u> clauses (as shown in the earlier discussion of adjective clauses). Furthermore, subordinating conjunctions sometimes introduce another kind of clause discussed below.

Complex Sentences with Noun Clauses

There is one more kind of dependent clause. Compare the pair of sentences below to determine how the underlined word in the first sentence and the underlined clause in the second sentence are used (subject, direct object, predicate nominative, etc.).

> 1a. Your <u>comments</u> may be held against you.
> 1b. <u>Whatever you say</u> may be held against you.

In 1a, *comments* is the subject of "may be held against you." In 1b, "Whatever you say" is the subject of "may be held against you." Now analyze the sentence pairs below to determine how the underlined word in each first sentence and the underlined clause in each second sentence are used.

> 2a. There is no excuse for his <u>actions.</u>
> 2b. There is no excuse for <u>what he did.</u>
> 3a. My parents know my <u>intentions.</u>
> 3b. My parents know <u>that I've been saving for a car.</u>
> 4a. We will give your <u>suggestions</u> careful consideration.
> 4b. We will give <u>what you say</u> careful consideration.
> 5a. The new president will be a careful <u>candidate.</u>
> 5b. The new president will be <u>whoever makes the fewest televised mistakes.</u>

The underlined words and clauses above are used as objects of prepositions in 2a and b, as direct objects in 3a and b, as predicate nominatives in 4a and b, and as indirect objects in 5a and b. So they are all used as nouns. **Clauses that act as subjects, objects of prepositions, direct objects, predicate nominatives or indirect objects are <u>noun clauses.</u>**

To check your understanding of adjective clauses, adverb clauses, and noun clauses, identify them below. Be especially careful on the last three.

> 1. The man whose car you hit has only minor damage.
> 2. I still have my wisdom teeth because I have had no trouble with them.
> 3. When he saw the ultrasound of his heart, he passed out.
> 4. The jury believed that the witness was telling the truth.
> 5. The computer that John bought does everything but wash dishes.
> 6. Austin has a cousin who looks just like him.
> 7. He knows if you've been bad or good.
> 8. What I don't understand is how you knew about the surprise party.
> 9. Do you know where you are going?

The subordinate clauses are identified below:

adjective

The man <u>whose car you hit</u> has only minor damage.

adverb

I still have my wisdom teeth <u>because I have had no trouble with them.</u>

adverb

<u>When he saw the ultrasound of his heart,</u> he passed out.

noun (d.o.)

The jury believed <u>that the witness was telling the truth</u>.

adjective

The computer <u>that John bought</u> does everything but wash dishes.

adjective

Austin has a cousin <u>who looks just like him</u>.

noun (d.o.)

He knows <u>if you've been bad or good</u>.

noun (subj.)   noun (p.n.)

<u>What I don't understand</u> is <u>how you knew about the surprise party</u>.

noun (d.o.)

Do you know <u>where you are going</u>?

The fact that a word such as *where* might be used to introduce adjective, adverb or noun clauses should emphasize the importance of looking for the use of the clause rather than trying to recognize clauses solely by cue words.

Omitting *that*

In the following sentences, how are the underlined clauses used?

He thinks <u>that you love him.</u>

The song <u>that he wrote</u> made the top forty.

That you love him is a noun clause used as the direct object, and *that he wrote* is an adjective clause describing *song*. What happens if, as is often the case, *that* is omitted from each clause as below? Do the clauses still have the same functions?

He thinks <u>you love him.</u>

The song <u>he wrote</u> made the top forty.

The functions of such clauses do not change, even if they look like independent clauses without *that*.

Verbals

Verbals are verbs used as other parts of speech. The three types of verbals are discussed below.

Gerunds

You may recall from an earlier discussion of parts of speech that a single word may be used as a different part of speech in different sentences. For example, in the sentences below, how is the word *left* used?

> He <u>left</u> his keys in the car.
> Her <u>left</u> arm is much stronger than her right.
> He doesn't know his <u>left</u> from his right.

As you can see, *left* can be used as a verb, an adjective, or a noun.
How is *running* used in the sentences below?

> 1. The dog was <u>running</u> across the street.
> 2. <u>Running</u> is good exercise.

Running is used as a verb in sentence #1 but is a noun used as a subject in sentence #2.
To name an action we often change the form of verbs to make them nouns:

verb form	noun form
express	expression
transmit	transmission
create	creation
compete	competition

Other times we use verbs as nouns. Recalling the earlier discussion of sentence parts (subject, predicate adjective, predicate nominative, direct object, and indirect object), decide how the underlined verbs are used in the sentences below. What spelling feature do all the underlined verb forms have in common?

> 1. <u>Diving</u> is his favorite sport.
> 2. His favorite sport is <u>diving</u>.
> 3. I enjoy <u>teaching</u>.
> 4. He gave the <u>painting</u> his best effort.

The underlined words are, in order: a subject, a predicate nominative, a direct object, and an indirect object.
All of these are noun uses. Notice that all the underlined verb forms end in -<u>ing</u>.
Verb forms ending in *-ing* and used as nouns are called <u>gerunds</u>.

Gerunds may also be used as objects of prepositions, as in the sentence below:

> She needs a lot of work on her <u>writing</u>.

Gerunds are one of the three kinds of verbals – verbs used as other parts of speech. (The other two will be discussed below.)

Find the gerunds in the sentences below and tell if they are used as subject, predicate nominative, direct object, indirect object, or object of a preposition.

> Your understanding increases with each lesson.
>
> The man suffered three broken ribs from the beating.
>
> During the trip we heard a constant rattling.
>
> The mayor will be speaking about voting.
>
> Her first career choice is marketing.

The gerunds above are *understanding* (subject), *beating* (object of the preposition), *rattling* (direct object), *voting* (object of the preposition), and *marketing* (predicate nominative).

Caution: Don't assume that every word ending in *-ing* is a gerund. Although every gerund will end in *-ing*, not all words with that ending are gerunds. In the sentences above, for instance, *during* is a preposition and *speaking* is part of the simple predicate *will be speaking*. Don't guess! Analyze!

Compare the gerunds in the sentences below. What is the subject of the first sentence? Is the subject the same in the second sentence?

> Eating is forbidden during the ceremony.
>
> Eating anything except vegetables is forbidden on that diet.

Eating is the subject of the first sentence. Obviously, *Eating* by itself cannot be the subject of the second sentence. What is forbidden by the diet? "Eating anything except vegetables" is forbidden. Therefore, that whole phrase is the subject. What does that phrase contain besides the gerund *Eating*?

As a verb form, a gerund maintains the properties of verbs. So in the phrase "Eating anything except vegetables," *anything* is the direct object of the gerund *eating*. The prepositional phrase "except vegetables" is also important because without it the sentence would say, "Eating anything is forbidden on that diet." Not likely. **Taken together, a gerund with its object and/or other words that complete it is called a <u>gerund phrase</u>. A gerund phrase can be used any way a gerund can be used.**

Find the gerund phrases below and determine how they're used.

1. Throwing the paper away was Bill's idea.
2. She has been making arrangements for moving to Washington.
3. Nancy liked being the only sister of three brothers.
4. This new process requires the combining of several chemicals.
5. My uncle's job is selling used cars.
6. My parents are looking forward to growing old together.
7. His hobby is rebuilding old cars.
8. She really dreads seeing her son's grades.
9. They were excited about winning the award.
10. Bicycling four times a week is lowering his blood pressure.

The gerund phrases above are "Throwing the paper away" (used as the subject of the sentence), "moving to Washington" (used as objection of the preposition *for*), "being the only sister of three brothers" (direct object) "the combining of several chemicals" (direct object) "selling used cars" (predicate nominative), "growing old together" (object of the preposition *to*), "rebuilding old cars" (predicate nominative) "seeing her son's grades" (direct object), "winning the award" (object of the preposition *about*), and "Bicycling four times a week" (predicate nominative).

Participles

As mentioned in the previous section, gerunds are verbs used as nouns. Let's look at another kind of verbal. Compare the use of the underlined words in the sentences below.

Are both words used as nouns?
> Crying is a good way to release emotion.
> The crying baby interrupted the service.

In the first sentence, *Crying* is used as a gerund (the subject), but in the second sentence *crying* is used to describe *baby*. Since *baby* is a noun, how is *crying* used?

Crying is an adjective because it describes *baby*. You can see, then, that verbals can be used as adjectives as well as nouns. **Verbals used as adjectives are called underlined participles.**

Find the participles in the sentences below:
1. The police car pursued the speeding truck.
2. After a disappointing evening, we were trying to keep our composure.
3. Our vacation, frustrating, expensive, and tiring, is not a fond memory.
4. Smiling, the doctor gave her the surprising news.
5. The blossoming tree is a magnolia.

The participles above are *speeding, disappointing, frustrating, tiring, smiling, surprising,* and *blossoming.* Hopefully, you didn't fall into the trap of labeling every *-ing* word as a participle. *Evening* is a noun, while *trying* and *providing* are parts of simple predicates. Remember to analyze the relationships of the words rather than making quick guesses. Compare the different uses of the underlined phrases in the sentences below:
> a. Studying harder will improve your grades.
> b. Studying harder, he finally made the dean's honor roll.
> c. Watching the movie, he fell asleep.
> c. Looking out the window, she saw a cardinal.

In sentence a. "Studying harder" is the subject and is, therefore, a gerund phrase (a gerund and a describing word). But in sentence b. the subject is *he,* and "Studying harder" describes *he,* so the phrase is used as an adjective and is called a "participial phrase." In sentence c. "Watching the movie" describes *he* and includes a direct object, *movie.* In sentence d. "Looking out the window" describes *she* and includes a prepositional phrase. **A phrase consisting of a participle with objects and/or other words that complete or describe it is called a underlined participial phrase.**

Find each participial phrase below and tell what noun or pronoun it describes.
1. The children playing hide-and-seek are my cousins.
2. Trying to impress the girls, Rick is always showing off.
3. We spent three days in Washington, seeing all the sights and taking photos.
4. They are looking for anyone knowing information about the robbery.
5. The auction, raising money for charity, will be held Saturday.
6. The man watching our practice is scouting for a major league team.

Notice that participial phrases may come before or after the word they describe, or may be completely separate and later in the sentence as in the third sentence. The participial phrases above are "playing hide-and-seek," "Trying to impress the girls," "seeing all the sights and taking photos," "knowing information about the robbery," "raising money for charity," and "watching our practice."

Since participles and gerunds can both end in *-ing*, it is necessary to analyze their use to identify both in the sentences below:

1. Wishing upon a star won't get you very far.
2. Wishing upon a star, Geppetto gained a son.
3. Understanding Greek takes patience and practice.
4. He eagerly awaited the dawning of the new day.
5. Changing the tire, he re-injured his back.
6. The council is seeking more support for reviving the celebration.
7. I am getting anxious studying for the exam.
8. Finding the door locked, he thought about breaking it down.
9. Leaving the country is an option he is considering.
10. Although scoring points is his forte, he is working on improving his defense.

The phrases are "Wishing upon a star" (gerund/subject); "Wishing upon a star" (participial/adjective describing *Geppetto*); "Understanding Greek" (gerund/subject); "the dawning of the new day" (gerund/direct object); "Changing the tire" (participial describing *he*); "reviving the celebration" (gerund/object of preposition); "studying for the exam" (participial describing *I*); "Finding the door locked" (participial describing *he*); "breaking it down" (gerund/object of preposition); "Leaving the country" (gerund/subject); "scoring points" (gerund/subject); and "improving his defense" (gerund/objective of preposition).

So far, we have looked at participles ending in *-ing*. Compare the underlined phrases in the sentences below. Do both phrases describe nouns or pronouns? Do both phrases begin with verb forms?

> Breaking the glass, Donna cut her hand.
> Amused by the comedy, we couldn't stop laughing.

Both are participial phrases describing nouns (*Donna* and *we*) and acting as adjectives. The difference, of course, is the form of the verb: *breaking* is called a <u>present participle</u>, and *Amused* is called a <u>past participle</u>.

If all past participles had one ending (as all present participles do with *-ing*), they might be easy to identify. Unfortunately, that is not the way our language works. Because of irregular verbs, past participles are formed in a variety of ways as you can see below:

> The wax, <u>melted by the flame</u>, ran down the candle.
> <u>Sung in harmony</u>, the song sounded much better.
> The picture <u>drawn by my sister</u> hangs in the den.
> <u>Set in Paris</u>, the movie depicts post-war reconstruction.
> We are looking for artifacts <u>brought here by early settlers</u>.
> The professor, <u>held in high esteem by his peers</u>, will be the chairman.

Find the participial phrases below – present and past.

> Startled by the thunder, the child ran to her father.
> The three missions flown by the captain gained important information.
> She shivered uncontrollably, caught without warning, frozen by icy winds.
> The campfire, left unattended, spread through the forest.
> Forgiven by his sister, he apologized to his brother.

Much of her fortune, spent recklessly, was not soon recovered.
We saw the statue, made in France and given as a gift to the United States.
The footprints found in the dry river bed may be from prehistoric creatures.

The participial phrases are "Startled by the thunder," "flown by the captain," "caught without warning" and "frozen by icy winds," "left unattended," "Forgiven by his sister," "spent recklessly," "made in France" and "given as a gift to the United States," and "found in the dry river bed."

Now try writing five sentences of your own with some present and past participial phrases, putting them in various positions. (Note: If you begin a sentence with a participial phrase, make sure it describes the subject. Otherwise, it is a dangling modifier, which will be discussed later in Sentence Problems.)

Infinitives

In our earlier discussion of prepositions, we said that prepositions (*from, for, on, to,* etc.) usually begin prepositional phrases that include a noun or pronoun as the object of the preposition. Compare the following sentences and see if they both contain prepositional phrases:

I went to France.
I want to go.

The first sentence does contain a prepositional phrase, "to France," with *to* as a preposition and *France* as an object. In the second sentence, though, how is *go* used? Is it a noun or pronoun and, therefore an object?

No. *Go* is a verb, so *to go* is <u>not</u> a prepositional phrase. ***To* plus a verb is called an <u>infinitive</u>, the third kind of verbal.**

You remember that gerunds are verb forms used as nouns, and participles are verb forms used as adjectives. Let's see how infinitives can be used. Compare the underlined parts of the sentences below. What part of the sentence is *money*? Is *to go* used the same way?

I want <u>to go</u>.
I want <u>money</u>.

Money is a direct object, a noun receiving the action of the verb; likewise, *to go* is a direct object, so it acts as a noun. **Infinitives can act as nouns.** What other noun functions do the infinitives have in the sentences below?

<u>To ski</u> is his only wish.
His only wish is <u>to ski.</u>

To ski is used as a subject in the first sentence and as a predicate nominative in the second.

Infinitives have other uses beyond nouns. Analyze the use of the underlined infinitive below by comparing it with the underlined part of the second sentence:

He was seeking a quote <u>to print</u>.
He was seeking a <u>printable</u> quote.

Both *to print* and *printable* describe the noun *quote*, so they are adjectives. **Infinitives can be used as adjectives.** But that's not all.

Compare the sentences below to determine how the underlined words are used.

> He left <u>to escape</u>.
> He left <u>quickly</u>.

Both *to escape* and *quickly* describe the verb *left*, so they are adverbs. **Infinitives can be used as adverbs, adjectives, or nouns.**

If we expand the infinitive above, we can see a similarity to gerunds and participles. What is it?

> He left <u>to escape the pressures of his job</u>.

The infinitive "to escape" is done to something, a direct object *pressures,* which is then described by the prepositional phrase "of his job." The whole infinitive phrase is used to describe the verb *left,* telling why and therefore acting as an adverb.

Like gerunds and participles, infinitives may have objects and other words that expand them into infinitive phrases, which can be used as adverbs, adjectives, or nouns.

Find the infinitive phrases in the sentences below and tell how they are used. Be careful not to confuse them with prepositional phrases.

> I fail to see the humor in that.
> The most important task was to repair the engine.
> To err is human; to forgive [is] divine.
> To my regret we lost the game.
> There are many things to see in Paris.
> His last request was to die with his boots on.
> I am sending a telegram to the commissioner.
> No one expects to be in an accident.

The infinitive phrases are "to see the humor in that"–adverb; "to repair the engine"–predicate nominative; "To err"–subject; "to forgive"–subject; "to see"–adjective; "to die with his boots on"–predicate nominative; "to be in an accident"–direct object. ("To my regret" and "to the commissioner" are prepositional phrases, not infinitives.)

Now try writing five sentences of your own with infinitive phrases in various functions.

Other Phrases

Appositives

What do the underlined phrases do in the sentences below?

Bill, <u>our top debater</u>, plans to go to law school.
I read a book about Clarence Darrow, <u>a famous lawyer</u>.
Amadeus, <u>a movie about Mozart,</u> won eight Academy awards.
The story was leaked by an official, <u>someone unknown to the governor</u>.
The lead actor, <u>Bogart,</u> starred in many movies.

If you said they describe, notice in the last sentence that *Bogart* doesn't describe, but renames *actor*. Look back to find the main word in each phrase: *debater, lawyer, movie,* and *someone.* Each of these is a noun or pronoun, which, instead of describing, actually <u>renames</u> a noun preceding it (*Bill, Clarence Darrow, Amadeus, official*). Notice that each phrase includes words and/or phrases that describe the renaming word (for example, *our* and *top* are adjectives describing *debater*; "about Mozart" is a prepositional phrase describing *movie*).

Appositives are nouns or pronouns that rename nouns or pronouns. Appositives may be phrases made up of nouns or pronouns, together with words or phrases that describe them.
Unlike predicate nominatives, appositives are not connected to a subject by a linking verb. Furthermore, appositives are not limited to renaming subjects. For example, in the second sample sentence above, "a famous lawyer" renames the object of a preposition, "Clarence Darrow."

Find the appositives below and tell what they rename:

We elected a new president, Don Sims.
My cousin, an honor student, received a scholarship to Harvard.
We ate at Pete's Cafe, a greasy spoon on Fifth Street.
We listened to one song, "Alone," a dozen times in a row.
Polio, a crippling disease, was once thought incurable.

The appositives above with the words they rename are as follows: Don Sims renames *president*; "an honor student" renames *cousin*; "a greasy spoon on Fifth Street" renames Pete's Café; "Alone" renames a song; and "a crippling disease" renames *polio*.

Now try writing five sentences of your own with appositives.

Absolutes

Analyze the underlined phrases in the sentences below and identify the main parts.

<u>His head swimming</u>, John pulled off the road and stopped.
She stared continuously at him, <u>her eyes reflecting her rage.</u>

The underlined phrase in the first sentence above contains a subject, *head,* and a verb, *swimming.* The underlined phrase in the second sentence contains a subject, *eyes,* a verb, *reflecting,* and a direct object, *rage.*

Thus, both phrases might appear to be clauses. Could the phrases stand alone as independent clauses, or are they dependent?

Both phrases are dependent. What makes them dependent? In other words, what would you change to make them independent?

The form of the verb makes the phrases dependent. To make them independent would require changing the first verb form to "was swimming" and the second to "were reflecting." But we want them to remain dependent to connect them to the rest of the sentence.

When a group of words with a subject and verb is made dependent by the verb form, it is called an absolute phrase (also called nominative absolute). Absolutes are common in literature but rare in conversation or technical, business, or academic writing.

If the absolutes above were made it into dependent clauses, they would take a different verb form and either a subordinating conjunction or a relative pronoun. For example,

       Because his head was swimming, John pulled off the road and stopped.

       She stared continuously at him as her eyes reflected her rage.

But absolutes may add flow and literary style and implied connections (instead of explicit causal [*because*] or time [*as*] connections.

To become more familiar with absolutes, find the absolutes below and notice the form of the verb.

       Michael, his voice cracking with emotion, read his resignation.

       We watched the moon rise, its platinum brilliance lighting the night.

       His spirit broken, the stallion submitted to the bridle.

       We sat quietly, our curiosity stifled, our interest dulled, listening to the lecture.

Notice that the verb form may be present participle *(cracking, lighting)* or past participle *(broken, stifled, dulled)*.

The sentences below also contain absolutes. How are they different from those above?

       Their faces bright with anticipation, the students awaited the teacher.

       The stereo played in the background, its music soft and reflective.

Neither of the two absolutes above contains a verb. However, we may think of them as having understood verbs (like the understood *you* in commands):

       Their faces *being* bright with anticipation. . .

       . . .its music *being* soft and reflective.

Try writing a few sentences of your own with absolutes. Remember, the verb form (or the understood *being*) should make your absolutes dependent.

Sentence Options

Writing classes and books often encourage a variety of sentence patterns. Actually, sentence content and purpose influence sentence patterns, as indicated in later sections of this book discussing emphasis, conciseness, and style. Sometimes short sentences are useful for emphasis, but several short sentences may sound like an elementary reader. Restructuring and/or combining sentences can be useful not only for variety, but for other purposes as well. Let's look at nine sentences that combine the information in these two sentences:

Sam got a high electric bill. He began to turn off more lights.

Notice the different structures below and think about purposes for the variations.

1. After a high electric bill, Sam began to turn off more lights.
2. Getting a high electric bill, Sam began to turn off more lights.
3. Sam, who got a high electric bill, began to turn off more lights.
4. His electric bill being high, Sam began to turn off more lights.
5. Sam got a high electric bill, so he began to turn off more lights.
6. Because Sam got a high electric bill, he began to turn off more lights.
7. Sam got a high electric bill; therefore, he began to turn off more lights.
8. A high electric bill prompted Sam to turn off more lights.
9. Sam's turning off more lights resulted from a high electric bill.

The first four sentences above may <u>imply</u> a connection between Sam's electric bill and his turning off more lights, but they <u>don't actually state</u> the connection. Implied connections may sufficient. All nine sentences may accomplish different purposes.

Sentence #1 focuses on the time factor with the prepositional phrase "After a high electric bill."
Sentence #2 begins with an action, which might get more attention.
Sentence #3 interrupts the main clause with another clause surrounded by commas, emphasizing *Sam*.
Sentence #4 begins with an absolute (see earlier section on phrases), which emphasizes *high*.
Sentence #5 indicates the cause and effect relationship between the two clauses with the conjunction *so*.
Sentence #6 also indicates cause with the first word, *because*, for emphasis.
Sentence #7 also emphasizes cause with *however*, surrounded by punctuation.
Sentence #8 indicates cause with the action verb *prompted* in a simple sentence.
Sentence #9 is the only sentence that doesn't end with *lights*. Instead *bill* is emphasized at the end.

The different effects of these sentences are subtle, and in the context of a story or other writing, a reader wouldn't likely be conscious of the writer's choice of sentence structure. But the writer's purpose would nonetheless be served.

Parallel Structure

<u>Repetition of Form for Parallel</u>

Understanding parallel structure will be easier if you are familiar with sentence patterns and parts of speech (see earlier sections).

What could you change in the following sentence to make it smoother?

> She likes swimming, bicycling, and to jog.

One way to improve it is shown below:

> She likes swimming, bicycling, and jogging.

The sentences above are an example of changing nonparallel structure to parallel structure. Let's examine it. In the original sentence, the gerunds *swimming* and *biking* and the infinitive *to jog* are used as direct objects. In the revised sentence, the infinitive was changed to the gerund *jogging*, making it parallel with *swimming* and *bicycling*. Or you could change the two gerunds to infinitives: She likes to swim, to bicycle, and to jog. **Most compound structures should be parallel, that is, repetitive in form.**

Change the following underlined compounds to make them parallel. You can probably do most of them quickly, but analyze the grammatical changes you make.
1. His usual pattern of studying is <u>to wait until the day before a test</u>, <u>to cram all night</u>, and <u>scoring higher than anyone else</u>.
2. The job consists primarily of three tasks:
   * <u>stocking the shelves</u>
   * <u>posting new sale notices</u>
   * <u>summary of sales</u>.
3. <u>More jobs</u>, <u>better education</u>, and <u>lowering taxes</u> were the main issues of the campaign.

Revisions below indicate the grammatical changes required for parallel structure (with explanations in parentheses):
1. His usual pattern of studying is <u>to wait until the day before a test</u>, <u>to cram all night</u>, and <u>to score higher than anyone else</u>.
(That revision changed the gerund phrase "scoring higher than anyone else" to an infinitive phrase to make all elements of the compound predicate nominative into parallel infinitive phrases.)
2. The job consists primarily of three tasks:
   * <u>stocking the shelves</u>
   * <u>posting new sale notices</u>
   * <u>summarizing sales</u>.
(That revision changed the noun *summary* to a gerund to make the compound appositive into parallel gerund phrases.)
 3. More jobs, better education, and lower taxes were the main issues of the campaign.
(That revision changed the gerund *lowering* to the adjective *lower* to make the compound subject into parallel nouns. Note that even though gerunds are used as nouns, changing *lowering taxes* to *lower taxes* makes the elements more similar, more parallel.)

Practice
Revise the nonparallel structures below.
1. Escaping his hometown and to find himself were his main goals.
2. When the rehearsal ended, everyone was angry, tired, and wanted to go home.
3. Gwen got the scholarship because she is imaginative, innovative, and a talented artist.

4. My job as a sports editor included interviewing for features, writing local pre-game and game stories, laying out pages, and headline composition.

Parallel Structure with Correlatives

As discussed in an earlier section, connectors indicate relationships between words or groups of words. What does *both* cause you to expect in the sentence below? Is there a problem?

> Sean is <u>both</u> intelligent and has a charming personality.

The conjunction *both* makes the reader expect an adjective parallel with *intelligent* following *and* (the second part of the correlative conjunction *both/and),* but instead we get a second verb with an object. How can we create parallel structure?

One way is to eliminate *both,* leaving simply a compound predicate:

> Sean is intelligent and has a charming personality.

Another way, more concise, is to eliminate the second verb and its object, leaving the adjective *charming:*

> Sean is both intelligent and charming.

Signals such as *both* can cause confusion when the expectation of parallel structure is not fulfilled. In the sentence below, what does the underlined signal make the reader expect? How can it be improved?

> Jan hopes <u>either</u> to get a degree in psychology or sociology.

Because the conjunction *either* precedes the infinitive *to get,* the reader expects another infinitive after *or* (the second half of the correlative conjunction *either/or),* such as,

> Jan hopes *either* <u>to get</u> a degree in psychology *or* <u>to pursue</u> a career in medicine.

But the writer meant "a degree in *either* psychology *or* sociology," a meaning which is clearer when the *either* is moved after the preposition *in* to connect *psychology* and *sociology,* the two objects of the preposition:

> Jan hopes to get a degree in *either* <u>psychology</u> *or* <u>sociology</u>.

In the sentence below, what does the underlined signal make the reader expect? How can it be improved?

> The book <u>not only</u> listed the members of the faculty but also their extensions.

Because the correlative conjunction *not only* precedes the verb *listed,* the reader expects a second verb after *but also* (the second half of the correlative conjunction), such as,

> The book *not only* <u>listed</u> the members of the faculty *but also* <u>provided</u> their extensions.

However, the writer intended the conjunction not to connect verbs but direct objects, *members* and *extensions.* This is better expressed by moving *not only* next to the first direct object:

> The book listed *not only* the <u>members</u> of the faculty *but also* their <u>extensions</u>.

When using correlative conjunctions, make sure the compounds (the words, phrases, or clauses to be connected) are parallel, and place each part of the conjunction appropriately.

In all the examples above, the correlative conjunctions connected words or phrases. What is the problem in the sentence below, and how can you correct it?

The price *either* comes down *or* the house doesn't sell.

The correlative conjunction connects clauses, so *either* must precede the first clause to be parallel:

Either the price comes down *or* the house doesn't sell.

Achieving parallel structure requires close analysis of what elements should be parallel.

Practice

Revise the nonparallel structures below.

1. The Wilsons plan either to vacation in Italy or France.
2. His classes are both provocative and with a flair for the dramatic.
3. You will either complete the work or you will receive an incomplete.
4. Not only did Jackie win the race but also set a record.
5. She has neither the time nor does she have the patience.

Repetition of Words for Parallel Structure

Another nonparallel construction results from expecting the reader to make connections not made obvious. Analyze the differences between the originals and revisions below.

1. *Nonparallel:* A teacher must work with students who'd rather be somewhere else and make the subject interesting and relevant.

Parallel: A teacher must work with students who'd rather be somewhere
else and must make the subject interesting and relevant.

2. *Nonparallel:* The student senate would like to find students who are interested in the project and select a committee to get started.

Parallel: The student senate would like to find students who are interested in the project and to select a committee to get started.

In the parallel revision of sentence #1, a parallel repetition of the helping verb *must* clarifies that the teacher *must work* and *must make.* Without the second *must,* the reader isn't sure who is to "make the subject interesting and relevant," the teacher or the students.

In the parallel revision of sentence #2, a parallel repetition of the infinitive form *to* clarifies that the student senate would like *to find* and *to select.* Without the second *to,* the reader can be confused about who is selecting a committee, the senate or the students.
Repeating a word is sometimes necessary to make parallel constructions obvious and clear.

In the sentence below, does *not* refer only to "allowing illegal payments to players" or to all three phrases? How can you clarify?

The new coach promised a successful program by not allowing illegal payments to players, emphasizing academic achievement, and promoting team involvement in campus activities.

As the sentence stands, there are three objects of the preposition *by:* the gerund phrases beginning with *not allowing, emphasizing* and *promoting.* One way to clarify that *not* refers only to *allowing* would be to repeat the preposition with each object, thus creating parallel structure:

The new coach promised a successful program *by* not allowing illegal payments to players, *by* emphasizing academic achievement, and *by* promoting team involvement in campus activities.

Of course, using one preposition for all three objects is fine if the objects are parallel and the meaning is clear; therefore, changing *not allowing* to *preventing* is another revision to create a clear parallel structure:

The new coach promised a successful program by preventing illegal payments to players, emphasizing academic achievement, and promoting team involvement in campus activities.

Always be careful that omissions don't cause ambiguity.

Can you find a problem in the following sentence?
    She believed that he was out to get her and she could do nothing about it.

That sentence can be interpreted two ways:
1. She believed that he was out to get her. She could do nothing about it.
2. She believed that he was out to get her, and she believed that she could do nothing about it.

Of course, the original sentence could be revised as in #1 or #2, depending on the intended meaning. Can you think of other possible revisions to get interpretation #1 and to get interpretation #2?

If interpretation #1 is intended, a comma before *and* would indicate two independent clauses:
    She believed that he was out to get her, and she could do nothing about it.
Or a semicolon would do the same:
    She believed that he was out to get her; she could do nothing about it.
If interpretation #2 is intended, a simple repetition of the relative pronoun *that* indicates parallel noun clauses used as direct objects:
    She believed *that* he was out to get her and *that* she could do nothing about it.

Practice
Revise the nonparallel structures below.
1. In the novel, the clerk knows that the money was stolen and he is the only witness.
2. A quarterback should know how to read defenses and be willing to sacrifice.
3. Mom empathized with the insecurity of Jan's job, the incredible hours, and the stress.
4. Jon quit after he concluded that he would never get a promotion, the boss didn't like him, and the experience wasn't particularly valuable.
5. We found sand on the bed, cabinets, and table.

Parallels in Comparison/Contrast

We naturally employ parallel structures when comparing and contrasting. Sometimes, though, a writer will unknowingly create nonparallel structures by omitting logical words. Analyze the differences between the original and revision below.

Nonparallel: Michael is as stubborn if not more stubborn than Hope.
Parallel: Michael is as stubborn as, if not more stubborn than Hope.

The addition of *as* makes the two forms – *as stubborn as* and *more stubborn than* – parallel in form. Omitting the subordinating conjunction *as* requires *than* to work as a conjunction for both *as stubborn* and *more stubborn,* which it cannot do *(as stubborn than?).*

In comparison/contrast constructions using *as . . .as* and *more . . .than,* (or similar constructions like *greater than* or *stronger than*), include the conjunction *as* to make the elements parallel.

Practice
Revise the nonparallel structures below.
1. Her class is as noisy, if not noisier, than any class I've observed.
2. In the recent election, the Democratic candidate seemed as conservative, if not more conservative, than the Republican candidate.

Completing Elements for Parallels

Other omissions can cause readability problems. Analyze the differences between the originals and revisions below.
1. Nonparallel: Education always has and always will be a priority.
Parallel: Education always has been and always will be a priority.
2. Nonparallel: My parents were surprised and interested in my artwork.
Parallel: My parents were surprised by and interested in my artwork.

In sentence #1 the addition of *been* makes the two verb phrases – *has been* and *will be* – parallel in form. Omitting the verb *been* makes *be* serve as the main verb for both *have* and *will, (have be?).*
In sentences #2 the addition of *by* makes parallel prepositions – *by* and *in* – for the object *my artwork.* Omitting the preposition *by* creates the unnatural *surprised in.*

Do not omit parallel verbs, prepositions, or other words if those omissions create awkward, confusing, or unnatural patterns.

Practice
Revise the nonparallel structures below.
1. My brother can and has thrown the discus.
2. Most of the class has knowledge and practice with the new computer program.
3. Chuck was familiar and concerned about the project.

Fragments

Compare the underlined parts with the rest of the dialogue below. How are the underlined parts of the dialogue different from the rest?

"<u>What time do you have?</u>"
"Six."
"<u>Are we going out to eat?</u>"
"Yes."
"Where?"
"Somewhere in Georgetown."
"<u>I'm looking forward to that.</u>"
"Me too."

From our previous discussion of basic sentence patterns, you may remember that a complete sentence includes at least a subject and a verb. The underlined parts of the dialogue above express complete ideas. Is that true of the other parts of the dialogue? It is common in dialogue to use phrases or single words. What about in other forms of writing?

Analyze the groups of words below. Which are complete sentences?

1. We worked for three hours on the project.
2. Having worked for three hours on the project.
3. Although we worked for three hours on the project.
4. A little imported car that had only 15,000 miles on it.
5. She bought a little imported car with only 15,000 miles on it.
6. A little imported car showing only 15,000 miles on the odometer.

The only complete sentences above are #1 and #5. The others are called <u>sentence fragments</u> because they are not considered complete, independent sentences. What do sentences #1 and #5 have that sentence #2 doesn't have?

Sentences #1 and #5 have subjects, but #2 lacks a subject and is therefore a fragment.

Complete sentences have subjects and verbs. (An exception is commands which have the understood *you* as the subject.)

Sentence #3 above has a subject and a verb, so what makes it incomplete?

The subordinating conjunction *although* makes #3 a fragment. It is a dependent clause without an independent clause attached. **Complete sentences contain at least one independent clause.**

What makes sentence #4 above incomplete?

Like sentence #3, sentence #4 lacks an independent clause. It begins with a noun phrase which is described by a dependent adjective clause. What word could you change to make #6 complete?

Sentence #6 has a subject and a verb, but the form of the verb *showing* makes #6 an <u>absolute</u> (see the earlier section "Other Phrases" for a refresher on absolutes), which by itself is a fragment. Change *showing* to *showed*, and the sentence is complete.

As indicated earlier, fragments are common in conversation, so we may carry them over into writing. Why do we use fragments in conversation as below?

> "Where did you go last week?"
> "California."
> "Why there?"
> "To see some relatives on our vacation."
> "Have a good trip?"
> "Not bad."

In conversation we frequently cut corners and avoid repetition. The above dialogue might be converted to complete sentences as below:

> "Where did you go last week?"
> "We went to California."
> "Why did you go there?"
> "We went to see some relatives on our vacation."
> "Did you have a good trip?"
> "It wasn't bad."

But in everyday conversation, why bother?

In much of our literature–novels, short stories, plays – we see such fragments in dialogue to approximate real speech. Authors occasionally purposely use fragments for other reasons, such as emphasis. However, **in academic and professional writing, fragments are nonstandard and should generally be avoided.** (Exceptions may include quotations and fragments for emphasis, e.g., Who believes his story? No one.)

Fragments sometimes appear unintentionally in our writing. We are so involved in the ideas we are expressing that we accidentally place a period between a fragment and an independent idea. In the example below, what would you change to eliminate the fragment?

> The big door swung open with a creaking sound. Its hinges dry from years without lubrication.

Replace the period between the two sentences with a comma, making the second sentence an absolute (discussed earlier in Phrases) and forming one complete sentence:

> The big door swung open with a creaking sound, its hinges dry from years without lubrication.

If in the process of writing we overlook fragments because we are concentrating on content, we may do the same thing in proofreading unless we look specifically for fragments. One way to detect fragments is to read the last sentence of your work, then the next to last, then the one before that, and so on. <u>Remember, fragments are not always short. Some complete sentences are short, while some fragments may be deceptively long and difficult to spot.</u>

Below are three sets of sentences, each set including a fragment followed by two methods of correcting it.

 1. The driver crashed into the wall. Having lost control on a turn.
 1a. The driver crashed into the wall, having lost control on a turn.
 1b. The driver crashed into the wall. He had lost control on a turn.
 2. We stood there waiting for hours. Because no one had a map.
 2a. We stood there waiting for hours because no one had a map.
 2b. We stood there waiting for hours. No one had a map.
 3. It was a very long trip. A journey through the wilderness.
 3a. It was a very long trip, a journey through the wilderness.
 3b. It was a very long trip through the wilderness.

Revision 1a combines the participial phrase with the independent clause.

1b adds a subject and makes two complete sentences.

2a combines the dependent adverb clause with the independent clause.

2b eliminates the subordinating conjunction to form an independent clause.

3a combines the appositive with the independent clause.

3b eliminates the needless repetition (*journey* for *trip*) and combines a prepositional phrase with the independent clause. You may be able to find other ways of fixing fragments.

Practice

Find and correct the fragments in the following paragraph.

  I thoroughly enjoy bicycling. Getting up at six o'clock every three or four mornings a week and riding twenty to forty miles with a group. My fellow riders are a strange mixture. A retired FAA man who rides twice a day and goes on two-week tours all over the country. A freelance photographer whose one-liners keep us chuckling. One guy is a basketball coach who secretly uses his allowance from his wife to buy new equipment for his bike. He eats nothing but beans and rice. Because they are high in carbohydrates. Another rider is a geologist who works in a bicycle shop because geologists haven't been in great demand lately. He recently had a run-in with a garbage truck. The truck having turned in front of him without signaling. A veterinarian, who's about sixty, rides with us between triathlons and doctoring animals. One woman on our rides is an elementary school teacher in her mid-fifties. Now recuperating from a shoulder separation suffered in a wreck during a hundred-mile ride with over 11,000 riders. A rider who used to race motorcycles and has his own bus and bicycle trailer with a capacity of over twenty to take groups to races. A woman who rode over 300 miles during a twenty-four-hour endurance ride is one of our younger riders. Not your everyday, run-of-the-mill group.

Comma Splices

In the sentences below, the variations of #1 are all correct except 1a. Notice that there are two independent clauses in each variation. What does that tell you about correct and incorrect methods of joining independent clauses?

 1. It rained all morning. We postponed the picnic.
 1a. It rained all morning, we postponed the picnic.
 1b. It rained all morning, and we postponed the picnic.
 1c. It rained all morning; therefore, we postponed the picnic.
 1d. It rained all morning; we postponed the picnic.

Sentence 1a is called a <u>comma splice</u>. Sentences 1b, 1c, and 1d show three ways to connect independent clauses.

Related independent clauses can be joined (a) with a comma and coordinating conjunction; (b) with a semicolon, conjunctive adverb, and comma; (c) or with a semicolon by itself. Independent clauses should generally not be joined with just a comma. **Combining independent clauses with just a comma is called a <u>comma splice</u> and is generally not acceptable.**

<u>Exceptions</u>: As shown below, comma splices are occasionally acceptable, but be cautious about using them unless you are confident they are appropriate.

Sometimes comma splices combine a statement and a question, called a tag question as below:
> It's your turn, isn't it?

Sometimes comma splices are acceptable with very short, parallel clauses:
> Musicians are not made, they're born.

This method is fairly common with contradictory statements. Of course, a semicolon or dash would work just as well and might be preferable.

Fused (Run-on) Sentences

Can you find a problem in the following sentence?
> Your biggest problem is punctuation it makes your writing unclear.

Notice that the sentence above contains two independent ideas (clauses) without no connecting word or punctuation joining them. This is called a <u>run-on</u> or <u>fused</u> sentence. **Fused sentences – independent clauses joined with no punctuation or connecting word – are not Standard English.**

To avoid fused sentences, you may employ the same methods mentioned in the discussion of comma splices. The fused sentence above could be easily connected by one of the following methods:
> Your biggest problem is punctuation because it makes your writing unclear.
> Your biggest problem is punctuation; it makes your writing unclear.
> Your biggest problem is punctuation, which makes your writing unclear.
> Your biggest problem is punctuation; consequently, your writing is unclear.

Practice

Analyze the paragraphs below to find fused sentences or comma splices; then, using a variety of the methods shown above, correct the problems.

> We went to the state fair yesterday, it had many new attractions. As usual, the carnival offered an assortment of rides, most of which were overpriced. The longest line was at the bumper cars I hate standing in line. I'm not sure a three-minute ride is worth a thirty-minute wait. Another long line wound its way around the Ferris wheel, the ride operator had to let people out two at a time, rotate the wheel and let two more out. The engineer who invented the Ferris wheel was G.W.G. Ferris, he should have developed a different way to

unload people. You'd think that in ninety years someone would have improved on the original Ferris model it was invented in 1896.

Next to the carnival was the midway, it had all kinds of gimmicks to get the customers' money. Some of the standard attractions were there, the ring toss was one of them. It looks easy, people think they can surely win a prize. Another sucker game is the baseball throw, every guy tries to impress his girlfriend by knocking over the bottles. No one succeeds, the bottles are metal, the base is magnetic. Others lose money shooting basketballs at goals barely larger than the balls, others get taken by the duck shoot. All the marksmen want to win teddy bears, they can't win using guns with tampered sights. Of course, all the macho men try to ring the bell with a sledge hammer, that will impress their girlfriends.

Subject-verb Agreement

Let's begin by discussing what makes words singular or plural. Although it may seem ridiculously obvious, what is the difference between the nouns in the two columns below?

house	houses
computer	computers
paper	papers
class	classes
boss	bosses

The first column is singular, and the second column is plural. The addition of *s* or *es* is our usual method of making nouns plural. Keeping that in mind, notice the difference between the underlined verbs in the two columns below:

He <u>sees</u>.	They <u>see</u>.
She <u>catches</u>.	They <u>catch</u>.
It <u>flies</u>.	They <u>fly</u>.
She <u>knows</u>.	We <u>know</u>.

Whereas we usually add *s* or *es* to make a noun plural, adding *s* or *es* to a verb makes it singular. This difference is important to remember in the following discussion. (Note: We change *y* to *ie* with nouns or verbs when adding *s*.) What pattern do you see in the pairs of sentences above with subjects and verbs if the subject is singular? What if the subject is plural?

Subjects of sentences must agree with the verbs in number; that is, singular subjects require singular verbs, and plural subjects require plural verbs.
On the surface that sounds easy enough, but several factors complicate the matching of subjects and verbs. Let's examine some of those factors.

<u>Agreement with Compound Subjects</u>
What if we have two or more singular subjects with one verb in a sentence, as below? See what patterns you can find, paying particular attention to the verbs and the conjunctions that connect the subjects.

1. John <u>and</u> Mike *walk* to school every day.
2. The Oak Tree Club <u>and</u> the Shady Grove Club *host* tournaments.
3. Alabama, Alaska, <u>and</u> Arizona *are* the first three states alphabetically.
4. The Smiths <u>and</u> Joneses *invest* carefully.

Notice that each sentence has two or more subjects joined by *and,* and all four verbs are plural. Two or more subjects are called <u>compound subjects</u>.

What patterns do you see in the sentences below?

      1. <u>Either</u> Jamie <u>or</u> Angela *wants* your book.

      2. <u>Neither</u> the newspaper <u>nor</u> the radio *uses* that kind of story.

      3. Susan <u>or</u> Jane *knows* the answer.

Notice that each of the compound subjects (*Jamie, Angela, newspaper, radio, Susan,* and *Jane*) is singular. **Compound <u>singular</u> subjects connected by *or, either/or* or *neither/nor* require a <u>singular</u> verb.**

Practice

Analyze the following sentences to determine the standard verb choice.

1. He and she (is/are) looking for the same thing.

2. Neither this school nor that one (has/have) a football team.

3. (Is/are) the secretary or an aide available?

4. Either the knight or the bishop (makes/make) a good sacrifice.

5. A child and a pet sometimes (becomes/become) inseparable.

The rule above regarding compounds subjects joined by *or* or *nor* applies with two <u>singular</u> subjects.
What if one subject is singular and one is plural? Analyze the sentences below and see what patterns you can find.

      1. <u>Neither</u> the principal <u>nor</u> the teachers *want* the schedule changed.

      2. <u>Either</u> the dogs <u>or</u> the cat *leaves* fur on the carpet.

      3. David <u>or</u> his brothers usually *work* after school.

      4. <u>Neither</u> the firemen <u>nor</u> the chief *knows* who started the fire.

In sentences 1 and 3 a plural subject follows a singular subject. In sentences 2 and 4 a singular subject follows a plural subject. Notice with which subject the verb agrees: the subject closer to the verb.

When a compound subject consists of singular and plural subjects connected by *or, either/or* or *neither/nor*, the verb agrees with the subject closer to the verb. So if the subject closer to the verb is singular, the verb is singular; if the subject closer to the verb is plural, the verb is plural.

Another factor in subject-verb agreement is verb forms for singular personal pronouns *I, you, he, she,* and *it.* Not all singular verbs are the same. Compare the two columns below:

      I <u>am</u> tired.   She <u>is</u> tired.

      I <u>have</u> money.   He <u>has</u> money.

      You <u>are</u> late.   It <u>is</u> late.

      I <u>find</u> time.   She <u>finds</u> time.

Although all these pronouns are singular, some of the present tense verb forms for *I* and *you* (called <u>first person</u> and <u>second person</u>) are different from the verb form for *he, she* and *it* (called <u>third person</u>). Consequently, even with compound <u>singular</u> subjects, your <u>verb must agree with the closer subject</u>. With this in mind, select correct verbs below:

      1. Neither Keith nor I (wants/want) to run.

      2. Harry or you (is/are) the best candidate for the senate.

      3. Either you or I (am/are) going to take the call.

In sentence #1 above, *want* agrees with the closer subject *I,* in sentence #2 *are* agrees with *you,* and in sentence #3 *am* agrees with *I.*

Now analyze the sentences below and generalize about the subject-verb agreement when both subjects are plural in a compound subject.

1. Trains, planes, and automobiles are popular toys for children.
2. Either boys or girls enjoy playing with trains.
3. Neither the churches nor the schools support the program.

When a compound subject consists of plural subjects, the verb is always plural. This is true whether the conjunction is *and, or, either/or* or *neither/nor.*

Practice
Analyze the variety of sentences below and select the standard verb.
1. Either your paper or mine (is/are) sure to win.
2. Neither the Smiths nor the Davises (plans/plan) to attend.
3. Either school or experiences (provides/provide) useful education.
4. The school board and the superintendent (has/have) to approve it.
5. Fans or an air conditioner (is/are) not really very expensive.
6. Bass and trout (is/are) fresh water fish.
7. Neither Mexican food nor Chinese dishes (appeals/appeal) to me now.
Now practice writing ten sentences of your own with compound subjects, mixing singular and plural subjects, using a variety of conjunctions.

Subject-verb Interrupters

Other factors can confuse you in making subjects and verbs agree. Find the subject and verb in each sentence below and see if they agree.

1. The volume of the instruments increases as the song continues.
2. Adjustment problems for every student are different.

In sentence #1 the subject *volume* is singular, so the verb *increases* is correct. In sentence #2 the subject *problems* is plural, so the verb *are* is correct.
Prepositional phrases (such as "of the instruments" and "for every student") that come between subjects and verbs may be confusing unless you recognize the phrases and remember that no part of a prepositional phrase can be a subject. Prepositional phrases always act as adjectives or adverbs.
Usually when they come between the subject and verb, prepositional phrases act as adjectives to describe the subject. Don't confuse the object of the preposition with the subject.

Likewise, don't let other interrupters confuse you, as they might in the sentences below. Identify subjects and verbs below and tell if they agree.
1. Schedules posted on the bulletin board are subject to change.
2. A student who lets social events interfere with studies is apt to fail.
3. A drop in oil prices, together with lower tax revenues, is going to hurt.

In sentence #1 a participial phrase "posted on the bulletin board" interrupts the singular subject *Schedules* and singular verb *are*. In sentence #2 the clause "who lets social events interfere" interrupts the singular subject *student* and singular verb *is*. In sentence #3 the prepositional phrase "together with lower tax revenues" interrupts the singular subject *drop* and singular verb *is*.

Don't let interrupting phrases or clauses confuse you.
Try writing five sentences of your own with interrupting phrases or clauses between the subjects and verbs.

Agreement with Indefinite Pronouns

Indefinite pronouns sometimes cause problems with agreement. Analyze the sentences below (all of which are correct) and make a generalization about the subjects and verbs.

> Anyone in this country has the right to petition.
> Everybody knows about her habit of gossip.
> Someone in the company is keeping the records for her.
> Nobody has any idea of the cost.
> Something in her smile attracts me.
> Everything appears ready for the parade.

Notice that all the verbs above are singular. **Indefinite pronouns consisting of *one, body,* or *thing* with prefixes *any-, some-, no-,* or *every-* are singular.**

There are several other indefinite pronouns. Analyze the subjects and verbs below to see what they have in common. The indefinite pronouns may be subjects or they may describe subjects. Either way the verb must agree with the indefinite pronoun.

> <u>Each</u> person *has* responsibilities.
> <u>Either</u> woman *deserves* the award.
> <u>Neither</u> child *cries* without a good reason.
> <u>Every</u> engineer *earns* over $40 thousand.
> <u>Each</u> *knows* the secret code.
> <u>Neither</u> *is* a suitable route.
> <u>Either</u> *has* advantages and disadvantages.
> <u>Each</u> of the candidates *has* five minutes to speak.
> <u>Neither</u> of the donors *wants* recognition.

In the first four sentences above, the indefinite pronouns *each, every,* and *either* function as adjectives to describe the subjects. In the last five sentences, *each, neither,* and *either* are subjects. **Whether used as subjects or as adjectives describing subjects, *each, every, either,* and *neither* require singular verbs.**

Now analyze the following sentences containing other indefinite pronouns and see what patterns you find. What determines if the indefinite pronoun is singular or plural? Notice to what word each indefinite pronoun is referring.
1. <u>All</u> the stores were closed for the holidays.
2. <u>All</u> the rice pudding is gone.

3. Are <u>any</u> of the green napkins left?
4. <u>Any</u> news is good news.
5. <u>More</u> couples are choosing not to have children.
6. The rain has stopped, but <u>more</u> is expected.
7. Were <u>most</u> of your friends at the party?
8. <u>Most</u> of the flour was shipped in fifty pound bags.
9. <u>Some</u> of my friends are consistently late.
10. <u>Some</u> reluctance is natural for first-time skydivers.

Notice that the verbs in sentences #1, #3, #5, #7, and #9 are all plural and that the underlined pronouns in those sentences refer to something that can be counted (*stores, napkins, couples,* etc.), but the verbs in the other sentences are singular with pronouns referring to things that cannot be counted. **The indefinite pronouns *all, any, more, most,* and *some* are plural when referring to something countable; these same indefinite pronouns are singular when referring to something as a quantity.**

Notice in sentences #3, #7, #8, and #9 above that the indefinite pronouns (*any, most, most, some*) refer to objects of prepositions (*napkins, friends, flour, friends*). Although a prepositional phrase may tell you if a subject is singular or plural, no part of a prepositional phrase can be the subject. Therefore, remember the earlier warning not to let interrupting phrases confuse you.

Agreement with *none*

Consider the sentences below. Do both sentences sound right?

> After three days of snow, <u>none</u> is forecast for tomorrow.
> Of the thirty students in her class, <u>none</u> is going to college.

In the first sentence above, *none* refers to *snow*, which can't be counted; therefore, *none* is a substitute for "no snow." In the second sentence, *none* could be read "not one student," in which case the verb would be the singular *is*. However, if *none* is read as "not any students," the verb would be *are*.

Most grammar books have traditionally considered *none* singular. But in conversation *none* often takes a plural verb when referring to something countable. Likely, no one will notice one way or the other, but using singular verbs with *none* is considered standard.

Practice
To check your understanding of indefinite pronouns, analyze the sentences below and choose the standard verb.
1. All the people in this class (is/are) on scholarship.
2. Every Sunday for the past three weeks (has/have) been overcast.
3. (Does/Do) either of the sisters have a date for the dance?
4. Everyone in the first three rows (has/have) a clear view.
5. (Has/have) any student answered all the questions right?
6. More of the cars on the freeway (seems/seem) to have bumper stickers.
7. When (does/do) most of the people arrive?
8. Each of these lessons (is/are) designed to improve your grammar.

9. Some of the exercises in aerobic dance (is/are) more difficult.
10. Anyone over eighteen (is/are) eligible to vote.
11. (Has/Have) any of the freckles on her nose disappeared?
12. Neither of the books (comes/come) in paperback.

Now try writing sentences of your own using the indefinite pronouns *each, every, neither, either, any, all, more, most, none,* and *some* as subjects or as describers of subjects.

Agreement in Inverted Order Sentences

Analyze the sentences below (all are correct) and find the pattern of subject-verb agreement. (Don't be too hasty in identifying the subject.)

> There are three kittens on our front porch.
> Where is the new telephone book?
> Here are the new spark plugs.
> Is there any hope of escape?
> Nowhere has he found a more compassionate person.

Notice that all the sentences above are in inverted order with the subject coming after the verb. The subjects are *kittens, book, plugs, hope,* and *he.* Sometimes inverted sentences cause confusion with subject-verb agreement.
When sentences are inverted, the verb must still agree with the subject, not an adverb like *there* or *here*, necessitating a further look into the sentence to find the subject.

Agreement with Predicate Nominatives

What might be confusing in the sentences below in choosing a singular or plural verb?(These sentences are all correct.)

> 1. Good winds <u>are</u> a sailor's biggest desire.
> 2. A sailor's biggest desire <u>is</u> good winds.
> 3. Computer chips <u>are</u> a big money-maker in Japan.
> 4. A big money-maker in Japan <u>is</u> computer chips.

In sentences #1 and #3 the subjects *winds* and *chips* are plural, but their predicate nominatives *desire* and *money-maker* (which rename the subjects) are plural. In sentences #2 and #4 the subjects *desire and money-maker* are plural, but their predicate nominatives are singular. When a singular subject is renamed by a plural predicate nominative (or vice versa) after the verb, a verb that agrees with the subject may sound awkward because it does not agree with the predicate nominative. Nevertheless, **a verb must agree with its subject even if it does not agree with the predicate nominative.**

Agreement with Clauses with Relative Pronouns

Analyze the sentences below (all are correct) and determine the pattern of subject-verb agreement. Why do you suppose that the subjects *who* and *that* are sometimes singular and sometimes plural?

1. Sandy is one of those people <u>who have</u> everything.
2. Bob is the only guy in our class <u>who has</u> long hair.
3. This is one of the books <u>that are</u> getting good reviews.
4. Mine is the only car <u>that has</u> whitewall tires.
5. Texas is one of those states <u>that have</u> a lot of pride.
6. In July this is the only one of the streams <u>that doesn't</u> dry up.

Notice that each sentence contains two clauses – an independent main clause followed by an adjective clause beginning with a relative pronoun (*who* or *that*) as its subject. Also notice that each adjective clause describes something in the main clause. In sentence #1 *who* refers to *people* and takes plural verb. In #2 *who* refers to *the only guy* and takes a singular verb. In #3 *that* refers to *books* and takes a plural verb. In #4 *that* refers to *the only car* and takes singular verb. In #5 *that* refers to *states* and takes a plural verb. In #6 *that* refers to *the only one* and takes a singular verb.

What the adjective clause describes determines if the verb in the adjective clause is singular or plural. **Relative pronouns *who, that,* and *which* may be either singular or plural. When one of these pronouns introduces an adjective clause, determine if the pronoun is singular or plural by determining what word the adjective clause describes.**

Now try writing five sentences of your own using the same patterns as those above.

Agreement with Collective nouns

Analyze the sentences below (all are correct) and make a generalization about the subject-verb agreement.

     The <u>team is</u> playing well this season.
     The <u>team are</u> getting into their cars for the parade.
     The <u>jury has</u> been out for five hours.
     The <u>jury have</u> not been able to agree on a verdict.
     This year's <u>committee is</u> very active.
     The <u>committee are</u> leaving the meeting one by one.

Notice in the sentences above that the same subject takes a singular verb in one sentence and a plural verb in the next. The underlined words are examples of <u>collective nouns</u>. **When they refer to a group as a single body or unit acting as one, collective nouns are considered singular. When they refer to the individuals or parts of a group, collective nouns are considered plural.**

To avoid awkward-sounding sentences (which the plural collective nouns sometimes create), you can change the subject to individuals or parts of the group. For example, change the subject of the last sample sentence above from a unit to individuals: The committee members are leaving the meeting one by one.

Analyze the sentences below and identify the pattern of subject-verb agreement. Why are the verbs singular?

     <u>A thousand dollars is</u> a lot of money.
     <u>Forty-seven points is</u> our school scoring record.
     <u>Seventeen miles is</u> the distance to the arena.

Notice that each of the subjects above, *dollars, points,* and *mile*s, is a unit (not individual dollars, points or miles), so the verbs are singular.

Now look at the sentences below, comparing each pair. What differences do you notice between the objects of each of the underlined prepositional phrases?

1a. <u>Two-thirds of the book is</u> fascinating.
1b. <u>Two-thirds of the students are</u> making progress on the writing skills.
2a. <u>Thirty percent of my check is</u> taken out for taxes.
2b. <u>Thirty percent of the voters are</u> first-timers.

The subjects above are *two-thirds* and *thirty percent*, and each verb is determined by the prepositional phrase beginning with *of* following the subject. *Book* and *check* can't be counted, so their verbs are singular; *students* and *voters* can be counted, so their verbs are plural.
Amounts, distances, fractions, or percentages are collective nouns, singular when considered as a unit. When the amount, fraction, or percentage is followed by an "of" phrase, the verb is singular if the object of the preposition cannot be counted, or plural when countable.

Agreement with Certain Singular Words Ending with *s*

Analyze the sentences below and, considering the form of the verbs, identify the pattern of the subject/verb agreement.

<u>Measles</u> sometimes <u>spreads</u> throughout a whole class.
In fourth grade, <u>mathematics</u> <u>was</u> her favorite subject.
<u>Politics</u> <u>is</u> not her real ambition.
The <u>news</u> <u>comes</u> on at six o'clock.
In most cases, <u>mumps</u> <u>requires</u> rest for a few days.
<u>Aerobics</u> <u>has</u> become an important part of healthful living.
Of all my classes, <u>economics</u> <u>is</u> the toughest.

Although all the subjects end in *s*, they are considered singular. **Diseases, sciences, and bodies of knowledge that end in *s* are usually singular and require a singular verb.**
To help remember this, think of *measles, mumps, hives*, etc. just as you would *pneumonia, flu,* and *chicken pox*. Similarly, think of *economics, politics, mathematics*, etc. just as you would *psychology, astronomy,* and *sociology*. All are singular.

Agreement with Nonsingular Forms

Analyze the following sentences and make a generalization about the subjects as singular or plural.

My <u>pants</u> <u>are</u> stained in three places.
The <u>acoustics</u> in this room <u>are</u> not good for soloists.
Someone's <u>scissors</u> <u>are</u> on the table.
Those <u>trousers</u> <u>fit</u> you well.

Are there singular forms of the *pants, acoustics, scissors,* or *trousers*? No. Even though they may refer to a single pair of pants, scissors, etc., none of these nouns has a singular form except *acoustics* (when it is referred to as a science). **A few nouns have no singular form and are always considered plural, requiring a plural verb.**

Practice

Select the correct verb in the sentences below, considering all the patterns of subject-verb agreement discussed above.

1. Every book (costs/cost) twice the former price.
2. Either inflation or unemployment (increases, increase) every year.
3. Most of the employees (favors/favor) improved benefits instead of a raise.
4. Her enthusiasm and curiosity (makes/make) her an excellent student.
5. (Have/has) either of the candidates offered a sensible program?
6. The administration (has/have) formulated several new policies.
7. His favorite pastime (is/are) eating and watching television.
8. Martin is one of those people who (keeps/keep) everything inside.
9. There (was/were) thirty applicants for the position.
10. If you haven't noticed, each section of the books (is/are) outlined.
11. (Does/do) most of the information in the articles make sense to you?
12. Somehow, neither the administration nor the teachers (has/have) noticed.

Pronoun-Antecedent Agreement

As pointed out in earlier discussions, pronouns usually take the place of nouns or pronouns. The words that pronouns replace are called their <u>antecedents</u>. Analyze the underlined pronouns and antecedents below, noticing if they're singular or plural.

> Each <u>boy</u> must pitch <u>his</u> own tent.
> <u>Neither</u> of the players brought <u>her</u> glove.
> Either <u>Jerry</u> or <u>Robert</u> will bring <u>his</u> lantern.
> All the <u>families</u> evacuated <u>their</u> homes during the flood.
> <u>Seventeen</u> of us received <u>our</u> grades, but four didn't.

In the first three sentences, the antecedents (*boy, neither, Jerry,* and *Robert)* and pronouns (*his, her,* and *his*) are all singular. In the last two sentences, antecedents (*families* and *Seventeen)* and pronouns (*their* and *our)* are plural. **Pronouns and their antecedents must agree in number. Singular antecedents require singular pronouns, and plural antecedents require plural pronouns.** Remember, because we frequently hear nonstandard usage, be sure to analyze rather than selecting the word that sounds right.

<u>Agreement with Indefinite Pronouns</u>

In the sentence below, is the verb singular or plural?

> Everyone <u>is</u> ready.

The verb *is* is singular. Since subjects and verbs must agree in number (and *everyone* does agree with *is*), is *everyone* singular or plural?

Everyone is singular. Thinking of it as *every one* (like *each one*) may be helpful.
How does *everyone* compare to other indefinite pronouns below?

> Anyone has the right.
> Nobody is immune.
> Everything was perfect.
> Everybody wants good grades.
> Anything is acceptable.
> Nothing angers her.
> Anybody has a chance.
> No one is at home.

All the suffixes, *-one, -body,* and *-thing,* are singular indefinite pronouns.
With this in mind, analyze the sentences below and notice whether the underlined pronouns and antecedents agree in number. Do not go by sound.

> <u>Anyone</u> in <u>her</u> right mind will vote yes.
> <u>Everyone</u> should bring <u>his</u> notebook.

The antecedents (*Anyone* and *Everyone*) and pronouns (*her* and *his*) are singular in both sentences above.

You may recall from earlier discussion about subject-verb agreement that some indefinite pronouns can be singular or plural, depending on whether they refer to something countable or not countable. Compare the subject-verb and pronoun-antecedent patterns below.

> <u>Most</u> of the manuscript <u>is</u> still in <u>its</u> original form.
> <u>Most</u> of the participants <u>are</u> sharing <u>their</u> views.

In the first sentence above, *most* refers to *manuscript* and is a quantity, not countable. In the second sentence, *most* refers to *participants*, which are countable. Just as indefinite subjects referring to quantity require singular verbs, **indefinite antecedents referring to <u>quantity</u> (not countable) require singular pronouns.** Likewise, just as indefinite subjects referring to number require plural verbs, **indefinite antecedents referring to <u>number</u> (countable) require plural pronouns.**

Agreement with Nonsexist Language

Conventional English usage for years was to use masculine singular pronouns when the gender was uncertain. Until late in the 20th Century, the pronoun *his* was used in sentences when the gender was indefinite, e.g., "Everyone should have <u>his</u> paper in on time." To avoid sexist language, some writers use the approach below.

> <u>Everyone</u> knows what to do with <u>his or her</u> projects.
> I hope <u>everybody</u> submits <u>his/her</u> application on time.

Using both masculine and feminine pronouns with a slash or an *or* between avoids sexist language but can be distracting (like a multiple choice test). Some writers avoid sexist language by alternating between feminine and masculine from sentence to sentence, as shown below.

Everyone knows what to do with her projects.
I hope everybody submits his application on time.

A less cumbersome, less noticeable approach are the variations below. What has happened to the pronouns and antecedents?

All the students know what to do with their projects.
I hope all the prospects submit their applications on time.

Both antecedents and pronouns may be made plural when it is practical.

Another approach is shown below. What has happened to the pronouns?

Everyone knows what to do with the projects.
I hope everyone submits applications on time.

The sentences above simply remove the pronouns when the pronouns aren't necessary.

Similarity between Pronoun-antecedent and Subject-verb Agreement

Compounds

Other pronoun-antecedent agreement patterns are similar to those discussed in subject-verb agreement. Compare subject-verb (s-v) and pronoun-antecedent (p-a) patterns below.

Jerrod and Ashley have completed their assignments.

Just as compound subjects connected by *and* require plural verbs, **compound antecedents joined by *and* require plural pronouns.**

Compare the s-v and p-a patterns below.

Either Sarah or Rachel has left her sweater.
Neither Tim nor Amos is answering his phone.

Just as singular subjects separated by *or* or *nor* require singular verbs, **singular antecedents separated by *or* or *nor* require singular pronouns.**

What if singular and plural subjects are separated by *or* or *nor* as below?

Either Richard or his sisters have to contact their parents.
Neither the students nor Mr. Hall has spoken his mind.

Just as the verb must agree with the closest subject, **pronouns must agree with the closest antecedent when antecedents are separated by *or* or *nor*.**

Collective Nouns

Compare s-v and p-a patterns below where the subjects (which are also antecedents) are collective nouns.

The team is having its best season ever.
The committee have disagreed in their opinions of the project.

Just as a collective subject referring to group as a unit (acting together) requires a singular verb, **a collective antecedent referring to a group as unit requires a singular pronoun.** Likewise, just as a collective subject referring to individuals requires a plural verb, **a collective antecedent referring to individuals requires a plural pronoun.**

Practice
Analyze the following sentences and select the appropriate pronouns.
1. I think everyone in the group knows what (her/their) goals are.
2. Either the union or the supervisors must change (its/their) ideas.
3. One of the players misunderstood (her/their) assignment on the play.
4. Apparently Bill and David are patching up (his/their) differences.
5. Neither the A-team nor the B-team has won all (its/their) games.
6. If a boy's experience is limited, how can (he/they) avoid mistakes?
7. Our class members have been working on (its/their) projects.
8. Because of the economy, a guy has to find work where (he/they) can.

Pronoun Case

Pronoun case involves making choices between *I* and *me, we* and *us, she* and *her, he* and *him, they* and *them, who* and *whom*, and *whoever* and *whomever*. Frequently people use what sounds right, which is often not the Standard English choice.

Pronoun Case for Personal Pronouns

The following analysis requires some knowledge of some grammar terms, which may necessitate looking back at the section on Sentence Patterns. Analyze the sentences below to determine if the underlined personal pronouns are used as subject, predicate nominative, direct object, indirect object, or object of the preposition.
1. <u>He</u> broke his racket strings with that shot.
2. The winner was <u>he</u>.
3. <u>She</u> and <u>I</u> put the puzzle together.
4. The oldest players were <u>we</u> and <u>they</u>.
5. Someone called <u>me</u> for a survey.
6. The director wants to speak with <u>her</u> and <u>me</u>.
7. The teacher showed <u>him</u> the problem.
8. We will not see <u>them</u>.
9. The last three weeks were the most difficult for <u>us</u>.
10. My parents gave <u>me</u> a car for graduation.

The underlined pronouns in the first four sentences above are either subjects or subject renamers (predicate nominatives): The pronouns in #1 and #3 are subjects, and those in #2 and #4 are predicative nominatives. The pronouns in sentences #5 through #10 are all objects of some sort: those in #5 and #8 are direct objects, those in #6 and #9 are objects of prepositions, and those in #7 and #10 are indirect objects.
Look at the three personal pronoun cases below and make a generalization about the cases of the pronouns used in the sentences above.

Nominative case	Objective case	Possessive case
I	me	my/mine
we	us	our/ours
you	you	your/yours
she	her	her/hers
he	him	his
they	them	their/theirs

Personal pronouns used as subjects and predicate nominatives are nominative case (sometimes called subjective case), and personal pronouns used as objects (direct objects, indirect objects, and objects of prepositions) are objective case.

If some of the uses of the pronouns sound strange to you (such as sentences #2 and #4 above), it is probably because you are accustomed to hearing nonstandard forms in everyday speech. Consequently, to choose between nominative and objective cases in your writing, do not trust what sounds right. Instead, analyze the way the pronouns are used in the sentences. Likewise, people sometimes use nominative case pronouns as objects, perhaps thinking they sound more formal. For example, someone might say, "The boss wants to see you and I," when it should be "you and me" as objects of the infinitive "to see." Again, do not go by sound. Analyze. Objects must be objective case.

Notice that **personal possessive pronouns do not have apostrophes.** The pronoun *it* is usually included in the lists of personal pronouns, and like the other possessive pronouns, *its* does not have an apostrophe. Whereas *its* shows possession, *it's* is a contraction for "it is."

Practice
Analyze the sentences below and select the standard pronoun case, nominative or objective.
1. Someone told (he/him) the wrong direction.
2. Both Amber and (he/him) have dated for two years.
3. The boys accused of robbing the store were Tim and (he/him).
4. I will ask Carter and (they, them) about the problem.
5. Fred came in after Joan and (I/ me).
6. Did you think it was (she/her) you saw at the concert?
7. The disagreement between Harry and (I/me) was resolved.
8. Sharon and (she/her) seem to be the best debate team.
9. No one could be sure it was (they/them).

Pronoun Case for Who, Whoever, Whom and Whomever

Analyze the sentences below and tell how the underlined words are used (subject, predicate nominative, direct object, indirect object, or object of preposition).
1. <u>Who</u> left the refrigerator door open?
2. The caller was <u>who</u>?
3. <u>Whoever</u> left this note can't spell very well.
4. To <u>whom</u> were you speaking?
5. <u>Whom</u> will the committee select?
6. We will support <u>whomever</u> you pick.

The first four sentences are simple. In sentences #1 and #3 *Who* and *Whoever* are subjects. In #2 *who* is a predicate nominative. In #4 *whom* is an object of the preposition. Sentences #5 and #6 are more difficult because of inverted order. In #5 *Whom* is the direct object of "committee will select." In #6 *whomever* is the direct object of "you pick." **Who and whoever are used as subjects or predicate nominatives, while *whom* and *whomever* are used as objects.** Like the personal pronouns mentioned earlier, these pronouns have cases:

<u>Nominative case</u>   <u>Objective case</u>
     who   whom
     whoever   whomever

Selecting the appropriate case is sometimes complicated when these pronouns introduce dependent clauses. When they do so, they are called relative pronouns. **Relative pronouns relate dependent clauses to the rest of the sentence.** (You may want to review the earlier section in this book on types of pronouns. Likewise, clauses are explained in the section on Sentence Patterns.)

The secret to making the standard choice is isolating the dependent clause from the rest of the sentence and determining the function of the relative pronoun in the dependent clause. Do that with the sentence below (#6 above). Find the dependent clause and look within that clause to see how the pronoun functions in that clause.

         We will support whomever you pick.

The dependent clause "whomever you pick" is a noun clause used as the direct object of "We will support." Within the noun clause, *you* is the subject, *pick* is the verb, and *whomever* is the direct object, requiring objective case. The inverted order (direct object *whomever* at the beginning instead of the end of the clause) may confuse you.

Given a choice between *whoever* and *whomever,* you might choose correctly for the wrong reason, thinking *whomever* is the direct object of "We will support." The impulse to look no further than the relative pronoun can result in an incorrect choice. How is *whoever* used in the sentence below?

         We will support whoever wins the primary.

"Whoever wins the primary" is a noun clause used as the direct object of *support.* Unlike "whomever you pick" in the earlier sentence, *whoever* is the subject in this noun clause.

Below is another example requiring close analysis of the clause. Choose between *whoever* and *whomever.*

         They will give the contract to whoever/whomever bids lowest.

Your first impulse might be to select *whomever* as the object of the preposition *to.* However, the whole dependent clause "whoever bids lowest" is a noun clause used as the object of the preposition *to.* Within that clause *whoever* is the subject and therefore nominative case.

If you are having difficulty with clauses, go back to the discussion of clauses in the section on Sentence Patterns. Recognizing clauses is, as you can see, important in selecting pronoun cases. The following discussion is even more complicated.

<u>Pronoun Case with Interruptions in Clauses</u>

Analyze the sentence below and determine why the underlined relative pronoun is nominative case:

         <u>Who</u> do you think will be the new chairman?

Who is the subject of the noun clause, "Who will be the new chairman?" so it is nominative case. That noun clause is the direct object of the main clause "do you think," which interrupts the noun clause.

"Who will be the new chairman?" is a noun clause interrupted by "do you think," which are the subject and verb of the main clause. As the subject of the noun clause, *Who* is nominative case. The noun clause is the direct object of the interrupting "do you think," making it a bit confusing.

Multiple clauses and interrupting clauses can be confusing unless you isolate them and recognize their relationships in the sentence, as well as the internal relationships within the clause containing the *who* or *whom*. With this in mind, analyze the sentences below. If you remove "Tell me" and the interrupting "you think" from each sentence, is it easier to see how *who* and *whom* function in each remaining clause?
1. Tell me who you think would buy such a product.
2. Tell me whom you think the convention will select.

In sentence #1, "who would buy such a product" is a noun clause, and without the interrupting "you think" it is obvious that *who* is the subject, requiring nominative case. In sentence #2, "whom the convention will select" is a noun clause, and *whom* is the direct object of "the convention will select." The inversion of the direct object *whom* before the subject and verb makes it even more difficult. Recognizing that *whom* is a direct object is easier by restructuring the clause: "The committee will select whom." Don't let interrupting clauses or inversions throw you.

Now analyze another sentence with multiple clauses. Set aside "I know" and consider the rest of the sentence. Is "you choose" an interrupter (like "you think" above), or does it have a different function?
I know whomever you choose will be qualified.

In the sentence above, the noun clause "whomever you choose" is the subject of "will be qualified," and within the noun clause, *whomever* is the direct object of "you choose." The noun clause is inverted with the direct object *whomever* preceding the subject *you* and verb *choose*. Everything in the sentence after "I know" is the direct object of "I know."

Practice
Analyze the sentences below, select the standard pronoun, and explain your choice.
1. They plan to hire (whoever/whomever) is most qualified.
2. Was it Mary (who/whom) you saw in Miami last month?
3. Is she the administrator to (who/whom) I should talk?
4. Ms. Davis wants to speak to (whoever/whomever) sends invoices.
5. I spoke to the clerk (who/whom) the secretary said could help me.
6. Please tell me (who/whom) you heard the finalists are.
7. She said (whoever/whomever) we pick will be fine with her.
8. (Who/whom) would you say is responsible for the error.
9. Dana plans to attend the lecture with (whoever/whomever) asks first.
10. Invite (whoever/whomever) you like to the party.

Pronoun Case in Elliptical Clauses

It is common in English to omit words, such as the understood *you* in commands (e.g., "[you] Close the door") or the understood *to* in indirect objects (e.g., "He gave [to] me the keys") or the understood *that* (e.g., She believes [that] he told the truth.") Can you find other understood words in the sentences below?

1. He is not as smart as she.
2. No one makes better spaghetti than he.
3. Rick likes ice cream as much as I.

In sentence #1 *is* is the understood verb of the clause "as she <u>is</u>." In sentence #2 *does* is the understood verb of the clause "than he <u>does</u>," and in #3 *do* is the understood verb of the clause "as much as I <u>do</u>." How are *she, he,* and *I* used in those clauses?

The pronouns *she, he,* and *I* are nominative case because they are subjects of what are called <u>elliptical</u> clauses. **Elliptical clauses that begin with *as* or *than* will often omit words. When personal pronouns are the subjects of elliptical clauses, they require nominative case.**

Do you suppose pronouns in elliptical clauses are always subjects? Do you suppose elliptical clauses always have only word understood (omitted)? Look at the sentence below.
> She doesn't like Jerome as much as him.

The elliptical clause "as much as him" likely omits two words, "she likes," (as much as <u>she likes</u> him) so *him* would be a direct object. **Whatever is <u>understood</u> (omitted) in an elliptical clause determines if a pronoun is nominative or objective case.**

People often do not use Standard English in everyday speech, so the speaker of the sentence above might mean, "She doesn't like Jerome as much as he likes Jerome," referring to someone else liking Jerome. Consequently, a listener might get a meaning other than the intended.

Pronoun Case for Appositives

What do you notice about the case of the pronouns in the appositives below? What part of the sentence does each appositive rename?
> 1. The captains, Don and <u>he</u>, will represent the team.
> 2. The culprits were those three schemers: Jan, Rosemary, and <u>she</u>.
> 3. My parents sent money to a needy student, <u>me</u>.
> 4. Mr. Willis introduced the artists, Sean and <u>her</u>.

In sentence #1 the appositives *Don* and *he* rename the subject, and in #2 *Jan, Rosemary,* and *she* rename the predicate nominative *schemers*. **Appositives that rename subjects or predicate nominatives require nominative case pronouns.**
In sentence #3 the appositive *me* renames the object of a preposition, *student,* and in #4 the appositives *Sean* and *her* rename the direct object, *artists*. **Appositives that rename objects require objective case pronouns.**

Practice
Analyze the sentences below and select the appropriate pronoun case
1. No one in the class understands algebra as well as (she/her).
2. Two good friends of mine, Donna and (he/him), helped wash the car.
3. You may run faster than (he/him), but you're not as strong as (he/him).
4. Shaking hands in the picture were two former rivals, Jo and (she/her).
5. We invited two teachers, Ms. Smith and (he/him).

Squinting Modifiers

Some grammar errors are distracting, so you want to avoid them to keep your readers from being distracted. Other grammar errors can confuse or mislead readers. You definitely want to avoid those errors. Probably the most problematic are vague referents, which we will examine now. There are four types of vague referents: squinting modifiers, vague pronoun reference, misplaced modifiers, and dangling modifiers. We begin with squinting modifiers

Do you see any problems with the sentences below?
1. Dee Linquent decided eventually to pay off the note.
2. The proposal that was considered last week apparently will be accepted.
3. Interest accrues on new accounts only on the first of the month.

The problems demonstrated in the sentences above are subtle and consequently often go unnoticed, sometimes with negative results. If you didn't see any problems, check the sentences again for ambiguity. Then look at the different interpretations below:
1a. Dee Linquent eventually decided to pay off the note.
1b. Dee Linquent decided to eventually pay off the note.
2a. The proposal that was considered last week will apparently be accepted.
2b. The proposal that was apparently considered last week will be accepted.
3a. Interest accrues on new accounts on the first of the month only.
3b. Interest accrues only on new accounts on the first of the month.

In the original sentences, the adverbs *eventually*, *apparently*, and *only* are called squinting modifiers. If the writer of such sentences is lucky, the reader reads it the way the writer intended. If the writer is less lucky, the reader doesn't know which way to interpret the sentence. If the writer is even less lucky, the reader interprets the sentence wrong.

Squinting modifiers are ambiguous adverbs or adverbial phrases or clauses, which might refer to what precedes or follows them. Squinting modifiers can usually be eliminated by moving them to different positions in the sentence.

The squinting modifiers in the sentences above are single words. Sometimes a squinting modifier may be a phrase or a clause. See if you can find them in the two sentences below.
1. The CEO said before the meeting he would consider all options.
2. She said when the speech ended she wanted to nap.

Depending on the meaning, the sentences could be restructured as below:
1a. Before the meeting the CEO said he would consider all options.
1b. The CEO said he would consider all options before the meeting.
2a. When the speech ended, she said she wanted to nap.
2b. She said she wanted to nap when the speech ended.

Practice
Find the squinting modifiers below and repair them
1. The movie that appealed to Rana tremendously bored Max.
2. The council advises patients regularly to check prescription dates.
3. He was certain by October he'd get a job offer.
4. The way she silenced the class completely amazed me.
5. Writing clearly increases readability.

Vague Pronoun Reference

Keeping in mind that pronouns usually take the place of other nouns or pronouns (antecedents), analyze the following sentences to determine the antecedents of the underlined pronouns.

1. Sharon asked Brenda if <u>she</u> was one of the nominees.
2. After completing the form with his pen, he put <u>it</u> in his pocket.

In sentence #1 does *she* refer to *Sharon* or *Brenda?* Similarly, in sentence #2 does *it* refer to *form* or *pen?* Who knows? The writer does, but not the reader. The antecedent is unclear. These sentences demonstrate a common problem in writing: <u>vague pronoun reference</u>. How would you remedy the problem? Try your own solutions before examining the possibilities below.

What has been changed in the sentences below to eliminate the vague reference?

Sharon asked Brenda if Brenda was one of the nominees.
Sharon asked Brenda if Sharon was one of the nominees.

Both revisions above eliminate the substitution of the pronoun by repeating the noun. Of course, the main reason for using pronouns is to avoid such repetition, but repetition is preferable to ambiguity. Are there other options? Examine the alternatives below to determine how vague pronoun reference is eliminated.

Sharon asked Brenda, "Are you one of the nominees?"
Sharon asked Brenda, "Am I one of the nominees?"

Changing the sentence to a direct quote clarifies and uses pronouns to avoid repetition.
Below are some other options to make the antecedent of *it* clear in sentence #2 above.

He put the pen in his pocket after completing the form with it.
After completing the form with it, he put the pen in his pocket.
After completing it with his pen, he put the form in his pocket.

Restructuring sentences is frequently the best way to eliminate confusion.
Avoid vague pronoun references by making the antecedent clear.

The examples above are vague pronoun reference within single sentences. Let's look at some vague pronoun reference problems in a group of sentences. Analyze the sentences below and determine how to eliminate vague pronoun reference.

Original - Will had two double-faults. He also committed three unforced errors. <u>These</u> caused him to lose the match.

First, to what is *these* referring – *errors* or *double-faults* or both? How would you clarify, depending on what the antecedent(s) is (are)?

If *double-faults* is the antecedent, you could move the last sentence between the other two:
Option 1 - Will had two double-faults. <u>These</u> caused him to lose the match. He also committed three unforced errors.
Or you could repeat the antecedent and eliminate the vague pronoun:
Option 2 - Will had two double-faults. He also committed three unforced errors. The double-faults caused him to lose the match.

If *errors* is the antecedent, you could switch the first two sentences and insert the third sentence next to *errors:*
Option 3 - Will committed three unforced errors. <u>These</u> caused him to lose the match. He also had two double-faults.
Or you could repeat the antecedent:
Option 4 - Will had two double-faults. He also committed three unforced errors. The unforced errors caused him to lose the match.

If *these* refers to both *double-faults* and *errors,* restructuring the sentence to eliminate the pronoun is probably best:
Option 5 - Will's three unforced errors and two double-faults caused him to lose the match.

As you can see, the original three sentences could be interpreted and misinterpreted several ways because of vague pronoun reference.

<u>Exception to Pronouns Replacing Nouns or Pronouns</u>
Do pronouns always take the place of nouns or pronouns? What is the antecedent of *This* in the sentences below?

We worked all day on the project. <u>This</u> resulted in a good grade.

This is not referring to a single word but to the whole idea of the first sentence – a common exception to the usual pattern of antecedents being nouns or pronouns.

Let's look at another pronoun with another broad antecedent. What is (are) the antecedent(s) of *These* in the sentences below?

She lost her job. Then she had a wreck. These were reasons for her breakdown.

In the example above, *These* does not take the place of a noun or pronoun but refers to the two preceding sentences. ***This, that, these,* and *those* may refer to one or more sentences and thus have more than one antecedent.** Multiple antecedents may result in vague pronoun reference.

Does the paragraph below contain a vague pronoun reference? If so, how would you correct it?

We worked for weeks landscaping our yard. We planted several saplings and shrubs. We created terraces with railroad ties and soil we hauled in. We made a path with large flat stones, carefully fitted like pieces of a jigsaw puzzle. This was difficult, painstaking work.

Does *This* in the last sentence above refer to the previous sentence or to the whole process of landscaping? It can be read either way. If *landscaping* is the antecedent (including the specific tasks following that first sentence), the ambiguity can be eliminated by repeating *landscaping*:

This landscaping was difficult, painstaking work.
If *this* refers only to the sentence preceding it, one remedy for ambiguity would be easy:

This fitting was difficult, painstaking work.

Practice

Revise the following sentences to eliminate vague pronoun reference. There will likely be more than one revision per sentence because of ambiguous antecedents.

1. The twins suggested to their parents that their bedroom should be remodeled.
2. Auditors examined the records of the companies to see if they had any irregularities.
3. He left the box in the cabinet which contained the tools.
4. There is disagreement with the property assessment.   This will affect approval of the loan.

Misplaced Modifiers (Describers)

As we've seen, placement of words, phrases, or clauses can make writing unclear. Do you see a problem with placement in the sentence below? How would you correct the problem?

> The green man's shirt was torn.

At first it appears that the man is green. The simple remedy is to move the adjective *green:* "The man's green shirt was torn."

Do you see a comparable problem in the sentence below? How would you correct it?

> We saw a genuine Chippendale cabinet browsing through the old bank.

The phrase "browsing through the old bank" seems to describe *cabinet.* Correct the problem by moving that phrase to the beginning of the sentence so it obviously describes the subject: "Browsing through the old bank, we saw a genuine Chippendale cabinet"

What is the problem in the sentence below, and how would you correct it?

> Increased surveillance should decrease crime which benefits everyone.

The clause "which benefits everyone" seems to describe *crime* but can be clarified by moving the phrase to follow *surveillance*: "Increased surveillance, which benefits everyone, should decrease crime."

What is the problem in the sentence below, and how would you correct it?

> The CEO demonstrated the increased revenues to board members using a graph.

The phrase "using a graph" seems to describe *members* but could be clarified by moving the phrase, as in the two sentences below.

> Using a graph, the CEO demonstrated the increased revenues to board members.
> The CEO, using a graph, demonstrated the increased revenues to board members.

As you can, sometimes you have more than one option for clarity.

Modifiers (descriptive words, phrases, or clauses) should be positioned so that what they describe is clear.

What is the problem in the sentence below, and how would you correct it?

> He left the file folder in the kitchen which contained all the contracts.

The clause "which contained all the contracts" should describe *folder,* but can be clarified by moving the clause to follow *folder* and surrounding the clause with commas:

> He left the folder, which contained all the contracts, in the kitchen.

Note: The commas are not Band-Aids. They are used to set off an adjective clause, discussed in a later section on commas.

Practice
Revise the following sentences to move misplaced modifiers.
1. I realized we had forgotten to read the minutes after the meeting.
2. John went to the door to let in the dog wearing only a robe.
3. Shattered by the fall, I picked up the pieces of the mirror.
4. I solved the problem that the teacher gave quickly.
5. She remembered she left her purse in the classroom after she got home.

Dangling Modifiers

The last vague referents are phrases that begin sentences. What is the problem with the sentence below, and how would you remedy it?

Obscured by poor English, you may not communicate your message effectively.

You might initially think that what is obscured is *you*. The remedy is not easy, but a couple of options would be "You may not effectively communicate a message obscured by poor English" or "Obscured by poor English, your message may not communicate effectively."

A dangling modifier is a word or phrase that begins a sentence and describes something, but what it describes is not clear.

Find the dangling modifier in the following sentence and repair it.

After examining the figures, arguments were heard for the best coverage.

Because the sentence above is in passive voice (subject receiving action) it is not clear who is examining the figures. Repairing the sentence could be as simple as changing it to active voice, inserting the person(s) doing the examining:

After examining the figures, we heard arguments for the best coverage."

Find and repair the dangling modifier in the following sentence.

By informing customers well in advance, they will have sufficient time to adjust.

It is unclear who is doing the informing in the sentence above. One remedy would be to change the beginning, dangling phrase to a clause: If we inform customers well in advance, they will have sufficient time to adjust. Another solution would be to change the subject of the main clause so that the beginning phrase describes the subject:

By informing customers well in advance, we give them sufficient time to adjust.

Revise a dangling modifier by making clear what it describes, which often requires changing the subject that the modifier precedes and sometimes requires restructuring the sentence.

Practice
Revise the following sentences to repair the dangling modifiers.
1. Without sufficient time to write, the assignment did not get a good grade.

2. Making an effective presentation, the proposal gained unanimous approval.

3. Bowing to public pressure, Saturday hours will be extended until 1 p.m.

4. Hoping to make her happy, my mother was surprised by my gift.

5. Optimistic and hopeful, his performance was a disappointment.

Punctuation

Commas

Probably the most difficult punctuation mark is the comma because commas serve many functions in writing. Think of punctuation marks as signals. Frequently commas signal pauses, but not always.

Commas with Compound Sentences

Analyze the pair of sentences below, noting the differences and finding the pattern of comma use. You might start by noticing what is on each side of the conjunction (*and, but,* etc.). For example, in the first sentence below, what does *and* connect? What does *and* connect in the second sentence?

        1a. The car stalled and caused a traffic jam.
        1b. The car stalled, and a wrecker towed it away.

In the first sentence, *and* connects the verbs *stalled* and *caused.* Notice that there is no comma. In the second sentence, which has a comma, does *and* connect just the verbs or more? What pattern of commas does that suggest? Analyze the following pairs to see if that pattern holds true.

        2a. I enjoy warm weather but not cold weather.
        2b. I enjoy warm weather, but I dislike the cold.

        3a. You might find the keys on the desk or on the cabinet.
        3b. You might find the keys on the desk, or your brother may have them.

Notice that the second sentence in each pair has an independent clause (a complete idea with a subject and verb) on each side of the conjunction, and the conjunction is preceded by a comma.
The first sentence in each pair contains the same conjunction as the second sentence, but that conjunction joins something besides clauses. In 2a *but* joins two direct objects, *warm weather* and *cold weather.* In sentence 3a *or* joins prepositional phrases, *on the desk* and *on the cabinet.* Those sentences require no comma.

The conjunctions in all the sample sentences above – *and, but, or* – are called "coordinating" conjunctions because they connect equal elements. Other coordinating conjunctions are *nor, for, so,* and *yet.*

A sentence with two independent clauses is called a compound sentence.
Compound sentences joined by coordinating conjunctions *and, or, but, nor, for, so,* and *yet* require a comma before the conjunction.

The key to applying this rule is to identify the elements on each side of the coordinating conjunction. A comma is needed if the coordinating conjunction connects two independent clauses.

Practice
Analyze the sentences below and place commas in the compound sentences.
1. The police broke down the door and rushed into the room.

2. The superintendent and the board of education met for three hours.

3. Winds are expected to be over 40 mph but no rain is forecast.

4. Be sure to take a coat or you may get a chill.

5. All the evidence pointed to one man yet the police made no arrest.

6. Everyone in the class but Anthony completed the test on time.

7. Firecrackers are prohibited in city limits but people still fire them.

8. The train traveled across the state and down the coast.

9. Make the best of each day for it may be your last.

10. She left no message nor did she indicate her destination.

11. We spent half the afternoon looking for something to do.

12. Neither the administration nor the faculty supported the program.

Commas with Introductory Adverbial Clauses

Analyze the following pairs of sentences, finding the pattern of comma use.   To begin, compare these sentences to those in the previous section on compound sentences: Are these sentences composed of two ideas? Are both ideas (clauses) independent? What is the difference between the first and second sentence in each pair?

>1a. Unless the weather changes, the game will start on time.
>1b. The game will start on time unless the weather changes.
>2a. When school begins, it takes time for some students to adjust.
>2b. It takes time for some students to adjust when school begins.
>3a. Because he burned the steaks, Dad took us out to eat.
>3b. Dad took us out to eat because he burned the steaks.

Notice that each pair of sentences contain the same two clauses, one independent and one dependent.   In the sentences with commas, which clause comes first? What does each dependent clause tell about the rest of the sentence? What kind of dependent clauses are these - noun, adjective, or adverb?

In the sentences with commas (1a, 2a, and 3a) dependent clauses begin the sentences. In 1a and 1b the dependent clauses tell under what conditions; in 2a and 2b the dependent clauses tell when; and in 3a and 3b the dependent clauses tell why the action took place in the rest of the sentences. Adverbs tell under what conditions, when, why, how, where, and to what extent; therefore, these are adverb clauses. **Introductory adverb clauses are followed by commas. When the adverb clause comes at the end of the sentence, no comma separates it from the independent clause.**

Commas with Introductory Participles or Participial Phrases

Analyze the following sentences to determine patterns of comma use. What kind of words or phrase precedes each comma?

>Disoriented, she looked at the compass.
>Amusing and surprising, the plays got rave reviews.
>Seeing the long line, we decided to try a later movie.
>Anticipating a delay, the officials alerted the patrons.
>Awakened by the alarm, he shut it off and went back to sleep.
>Seen from a distance, the sculpture looked like a real person.

The sentences above begin with participles or participial phrases, each followed by a comma. **Introductory participial phrases are followed by commas.**

No Commas with Introductory Gerunds or Gerund Phrases

Gerunds are sometimes confused with participles because gerunds end with *ing*, and so do many participles. In the sentences below, why would you not use commas after the gerund or gerund phrase?

> Packing took most of the day.
> Changing schools can be a difficult adjustment.

The gerund and gerund phrase are used as subjects in the sentences above, and you wouldn't separate subject and verb with a comma. **Gerunds and gerund phrases are generally not separated with commas.**

Commas with Introductory Infinitives or Infinitive Phrases

Analyze the sentences below to determine comma patterns with infinitives. How is each infinitive used in the sentence? Why do you suppose commas follow some infinitive phrases but not others?

> 1. To know him is to love him.
> 2. To increase productivity, the company installed new computers.
> 3. To improve his reading comprehension is his primary goal.
> 4. To find the missing child, the police began a massive search.

In sentences #1 and #3 the infinitive phrases are subjects, which should not be separated by commas from the verbs. In sentences #2 and #4 the infinitive phrases are used as adverbs to describe (telling why) and are set off by commas. **Introductory infinitives or infinitive phrases used to describe are usually followed by commas; infinitives or infinitive phrases used as subjects are not set off by commas.**

Commas with Introductory Prepositional Phrases

Analyze the sentences below to determine comma patterns with introductory prepositional phrases. (Hint: the difference is simpler than you might imagine.)

> 1a. For her brother she bought a new camera.
> 1b. For anyone seeking a new job, a good resume is important.
> 2a. Until yesterday I had never seen a live dolphin.
> 2b. Until the end of the month, we'll have to cut expenses.
> 3a. After the exam we all went to Donnie's to relax.
> 3b. After weeks of intensive training in lifesaving, he was promoted and reassigned.

The first sentence in each pair above contains a short prepositional phrase, which is not set off with a comma. The second sentence in each pair begins with a long prepositional phrase (or more than one) followed by a comma. **Lengthy introductory prepositional phrases are usually followed by commas; short, single prepositional phrases are usually not followed by commas unless they might be read incorrectly without a comma.**

Exceptions
Exception 1. Below are two sentences that are exceptions to the usual rule of following long introductory prepositional phrases with commas. Analyze them to see why they contain no commas.

After a lengthy aerobic workout is my favorite time to drink a soda.
Across the silent desert plain swept a howling wind.

Notice that each sentence above is turned around (inverted); that is, a prepositional phrase and verb come before the subject. Even with lengthy prepositional phrases, no comma is used in such inverted sentences.

Exception 2. Below are two sentences that are exceptions to the usual rule of not following short, single prepositional phrases with commas. How could they be misread, and how would you correct them?

In the morning classes at our school begin at 8:30.
To teach elementary school teachers need plenty of patience.

Readers might first read "morning classes" together as if *morning* describes *classes*. Similarly we might read "school teachers" together as if *school* describes *teachers*. To avoid misreading, a comma is often required between the introductory phrase and the rest of the sentence:

In the morning, classes at our school begin at 8:30.
To teach elementary school, teachers need plenty of patience.

Commas with Absolutes

See the section on absolutes if you don't remember them. What pattern of comma use do you see in the sentences below?

Her heart broken, she cried ceaselessly for days.
He wore a forced smile, his real feelings betrayed by his eyes.
Jack, his nimbleness diminished with age, tripped over the candlestick.

All three sentences contain absolutes, and whether they begin or end a sentence or come in the middle, **use commas to separate absolutes.**

Practice
Analyze the sentences below and place commas where appropriate.
1. When the whistle blows work stops immediately.
2. After September the weather will get cooler.
3. Her trance broken, she could not remember anything she'd done.
4. On a small island in the Pacific is a hermit from my home town.
5. Because the meeting ended we were able to attend the concert.
6. To find the puppy a home took a whole afternoon.
7. Seeing his way blocked the halfback skirted the end for a score.
8. Attending his first recital was a real treat for Walt.
9. From Dallas we received an offer for an audition.
10. A fire can quickly get out of control if you are not careful.
11. Without any warning or preparation she gave an interesting talk.
12. If no one calls Mary will keep the kitten she found.
13. His head throbbing, he took two aspirin and lay down.
14. Flying over Hawaii I was impressed with the clear water.
15. In our newspaper ads cost only two dollars for twenty words.
16. We will try the next applicant since this one is not qualified.
17. To keep his car in top condition he washes and waxes it weekly.

Commas in Series

Analyze the sentences below to determine the comma patterns.

> A baseball, a glove, a bat, and a catcher's mask were in the bag.
> On this diet you can't eat meat, cheese, or other dairy products.
> He had three injuries: a bruised thigh, a twisted ankle, and a stubbed toe.
> Her cousins, aunt, and uncle visited for the weekend.
> Bring me a book, a magazine, or a journal to read on the trip.
> Dirty clothes were on the floor, under the bed, and on the doorknob.

Each sentence above contains a series. Whether in a series of subjects, complements, clauses, or phrases, **commas usually come between each item in a series.**

Possible Series Exception: Oxford Comma

The comma before the conjunction in a series, often called the Oxford Comma, is optional in most cases, except in journalism, in which it is normally omitted, or in cases where omitting the comma might be misleading, such as the following sentences. What difference does the comma make in the sentences below? (Hint: How many different skirts?)

1. The skirts come in assorted colors: red and yellow, blue and green, orange and gray, black and white.
2. The skirts come in assorted colors: red and yellow, blue and green, orange and gray, black, and white.

Without the comma before the last *and*, sentence #1 seems to offer four different skirts. With the comma, though, sentence #2 definitely offers five different skirts. If the writer intends five different skirts, sentence #1 might be read wrong.

Commas with Coordinate Adjectives (Special Type of Series)

Notice how commas are used with a series of two or more adjectives below:

> His amiable, jovial, vulnerable face helps him make friends quickly.
> The novel weaves a mysterious, bizarre tale in the Berkshires.

Notice that commas in the first sentence above separate the adjectives *amiable, jovial,* and *vulnerable* from each other but not from the word they describe, *face.* Likewise, in the second sentence a comma separates the adjectives *mysterious* and *bizarre* from each other but not from the word they describe, *tale.* Could the adjectives be switched around (e.g., "a bizarre, mysterious tale")? Yes.
Adjectives that can be switched (called <u>coordinate adjectives</u>) are separated with commas.

Another way of recognizing coordinate adjectives is that you could put *and* between them (e.g., "a bizarre <u>and</u> mysterious tale").

Are the underlined adjectives in the sentence below coordinate adjectives? Could they be switched with each other or have *and* between them?

> We had our <u>usual chef</u> salad for lunch.

Even though *usual* and *chef* are adjectives, we consider "chef salad" as a unit; therefore, *usual* is treated as a single adjective describing that unit. You would not put *and* between the two adjectives, nor could you switch them ("chef usual salad").

Commas with Appositives

Analyze the sentences below to determine the pattern of commas.

> We bought our tickets for Brazil, our vacation paradise.
> He gave the waiter, a cheerful chap, four dollars for a tip.
> Dr. Martin, her gynecologist, says she needs more iron.
> No one deserves a raise more than Bobbie, the office manager.

The phrases "our vacation paradise," "a cheerful chap," "her gynecologist," and "the office manager" are all appositives. **Appositives are often* set off with commas from the rest of the sentence.**
*The next section on nonessential vs. essential appositives will demonstrate exceptions to this rule, followed by a similar pattern for clauses.

Practice

Place commas where necessary in the following sentences.
1. In the summer I do a lot of sunbathing my favorite outdoor sport.
2. A short stocky man entered the room sat in the corner and went to sleep.
3. Pushing with all his might he finally moved the car off the road.
4. Sometimes when the moon is just right he says his facial hair grows.
5. No one knows for sure but everyone thinks he's a closet audiophile.
6. She pushed her way into the group even though she wasn't welcome.
7. If you don't mind I'd rather figure it out for myself.
8. The old man a regular customer at the cafe never looked at a menu.
9. The music was languid soothing and almost transcendental.
10. Sports our national preoccupation can be beneficial in moderation.

Commas with Nonessential Appositives

Why do you suppose the appositive in the first sentence below is set off by commas and the appositive in the second sentence isn't? (Clue: How many first attempts at poetry does Jeff have, and how many poems does Poe have?)

> Jeff's first attempt at poetry, "The Bulls," is about life on a ranch.
> Edgar Allan Poe's poem "The Bells" uses onomatopoeia.

Because Poe wrote many poems, "The Bells" is essential to identify which Poe poem is being discussed. **Essential (also called *restrictive*) appositives <u>are not</u> set off by commas.** In contrast, Jeff could have only one first attempt at poetry, so "The Bulls" is not essential to indicate which of his poems is being discussed. **Nonessential (also called nonrestrictive) appositives <u>are</u> set off by commas.**

Commas with Nonessential Clauses

Do you suppose the same comma pattern applies with nonessential clauses as with nonessential appositives? Compare the two sentences below. Is the underlined clause essential or unessential? (Read each sentence without the underlined clause to see if it makes any difference in the meaning.)

> He doesn't like people <u>who lie.</u>
> Susan's father, <u>who is a mechanic,</u> works on her car.

If you remove "who lie," it changes the meaning of the first sentence, so the clause is essential. **Essential clauses are <u>not</u> set off by commas.** However, removing "who is a mechanic" does not change the meaning of the second sentence but is merely additional information—interesting or useful, perhaps, but not essential for the meaning of the sentence. **Nonessential clauses <u>are</u> set off by commas.**

Commas with Dates

Comparing the following sentences, what patterns of comma use do you see?

> He graduated on May 15, 1998, with a degree in engineering.
> They spent Thursday, January 14, in Toledo.
> The show is scheduled for Saturday, Oct. 19, 2002, in Los Angeles.
> An audit on 23 September 2001 showed some discrepancies.
> He graduated in May 1998 with a degree in engineering.
> Her birthday is March 8th.

Use commas to separate items in dates as follows: between the day of the month and the year (unless the day precedes the month); between the day of the week and the month; at the end of the date if commas are used between earlier parts of that date. Do not use commas to separate merely a month from a year or a day from a month.

Commas in Addresses

What pattern of comma use do you see in the sentences below?

> The Annual Pancake Parade in Liberal, Kansas, draws a big crowd.
> We flew to London, England, for a two-week vacation.
> He lived at 1234 Boardwalk Ave., Norman, OK 73069, for ten years.

Use commas to separate cities and states or cities and countries.
Use commas to separate items in an address (except between state and zip code).
Use commas at the end of an address if commas are used elsewhere in the address.

Commas with Introductory Words and Expressions

What pattern of comma use do you see in the sentences below?

> Well, have you found the solution to the problem?
> No, I haven't figured it out.
> Yes, my hair is green.
> Why, it was only yesterday that you joined the firm.
> By the way, the landlord said your rent is overdue.
> Of course, no theory is universally accepted.

Each sentence above begins with an introductory word or expression. **Use commas after introductory words and expressions.**

Commas with Transition Words

What pattern of comma use do you see in the sentences below?

> I'm sure, however, that chewing gum contributes to cavities.
> Consequently, the war was over before expected.
> The expression did, in fact, originate in the fifteenth century.
> In other words, he can't chew gum and walk at the same time.
> The Rangers, for example, have never won a pennant.

Each sentence above has a conjunctive adverb or phrase. **Use commas to set off conjunctive adverbs or phrases (sometimes called transition words or phrases).**

Commas with Direct Addresses

What pattern of comma use do you see in the sentences below?

      Mr. Wilkerson, can you rephrase that question?

      Amber, you were selected as the outstanding writer.

      I know you aren't happy with my grades, Mom.

      I'm sure, Lance, that you will succeed.

Each sentence above addresses someone, whether at the beginning, middle, or end of the sentence. **Use commas to set off direct addresses (calling a person by name, title, etc.).**

Commas with Contrasting Phrases

What pattern of comma use do you see in the sentences below?

      The movie has a happy ending, unlike the book.

      She asked for money from her mom, not her dad.

      Brett spent my money, not his, on the new CD.

Phrases like "unlike the book," "not her dad," and "not his" are called <u>contrasting phrases</u>. **Use commas to separate contrasting phrases.**

Commas with Tag Questions

What pattern of comma use do you see in the sentences below?

      You spent the entire afternoon watching cartoons, didn't you?

      You're the new chairman, aren't you?

      She doesn't want to sell the house, does she?

Sometimes we end sentences with questions that imply information from earlier in the sentences. These are called tag questions. **Use commas to separate tag questions.**

Commas with Omissions

What pattern of comma use do you see in the sentences below?

      Jeff is the taller of the two brothers; Jack, the smarter.

      The girls took the subway; the boys, the taxi.

      To err is human; to forgive, divine.

Notice that after the semicolon in each sentence above, a comma replaces the implied verb (*is, took,* and *is*). **Use a comma to indicate the omission of a repeated verb.**

Commas with Names and Titles

What pattern of comma use do you see in the sentences below?

> We met Susan Coltrane, Ph.D., at a conference in Boston.
> She introduced Dr. Susan Coltrane as the new department head.
> David Hart, D.D.S., was named Dentist of the Year.

In the first and third sentences above, the person's title (Ph.D. and D.D.S.) follows her or his name and is set off by commas. In the second sentence the title precedes the name, so there is no comma. Use commas to separate a person's title or degree from the rest of the sentence when the title or degree follows the person's name.

Commas with Parenthetical Comments

What pattern of comma use do you see in the sentences below?

> The sun, according to one myth, is awakened by the rooster's crow.
> The governor's answer, like most of his responses, was vague.
> Many spiders, as you know, are not poisonous.

All three sentences above have what are called parenthetical comments. **You may sometimes use commas (instead of parentheses) to set off a parenthetical comment that you want to keep in the flow of the sentence.**

Commas with Direct Quotations

What pattern of comma use do you see in the sentences below?

> "Make sure you send the check to the right address," said John.
> My mother asked, "What time did you get home last night?"

In both sentences above, commas come between the quotation and the speaker and verb. **Use commas to separate direct quotations from the speaker and verb.**

Notice how this rule applies in the sentence below when the speaker and verb interrupt a one sentence quotation.

> "If you look closely to the north," Avery said, "you'll see the satellite."
> "Yes," she replied, "the moon is full and so am I."

In both sentences commas separate each part of the quotation from the speaker and verb. (Notice that the second part of the quotation does not begin with a capital, indicating the continuation of the quotation.) **When a direct quotation of one sentence is interrupted by a speaker and verb, separate both parts of the quotation with commas.**

How does the punctuation and capitalization of the sentence below vary from the one above? Why do you suppose?

> "Look closely to the north," Avery said. "You'll see the satellite."

Notice that the speaker and verb come between two <u>separate sentences</u>; therefore, a period follows the verb *said,* and the sentence after the subject and verb begins with a capital.

Colons

Chief Colon Function

Analyze the sentences below and see what pattern you can find for using colons. What follows each colon?
1. I looked everywhere for the paper: on the desk, under the bed, in the closet, and in the trash can.
2. Bring the proper gear: a raincoat, a backpack, a mess kit, a sleeping bag, and knife.
3. She had all the symptoms: nausea, headache, muscle aches, and fever.

Notice that each colon above introduces a series. **The chief function of the colon is to introduce. Colons often introduce series.**

What do the colons introduce in the following sentences?
1. He outlined his plan: a step-by-step remodeling of the building.
2. My sister had a great idea: sell raffle tickets to raise the money.
3. The research yielded one surprise: females outnumbered males.
4. She insisted on one condition: No one could get a refund.
5. I'll give you an example: three students failed every section.

In the sentences above, information after each colon explains, exemplifies, illustrates, or summarizes something that precedes the colon (*plan, idea, surprise, condition, example*). **Colons can introduce explanatory information.** If that information comes in the form of an independent clause, as in sentences #4 and #5 above, what do you notice about capitalization?

The colons in both #4 and #5 are followed by complete sentences (independent clauses), but in sentence #4 the sentence following the colon is capitalized, and in #5 the sentence following the colon is not capitalized. **An independent clause following a colon may begin with either a capital or a lower-case letter.**

What do the colons introduce in the following sentences?
1. Students know the first part of the Gettysburg Address: "Four score and seven years ago. . ."
2. The principal gave a short statement: "We will not tolerate disrespect for teachers from any student."

Both sentences above begin with statements that introduce quotations with colons. **Colons can introduce formal statements or quotations.**

In all the examples of colons above notice what comes before the colon, regardless of what follows the colon. Each colon is preceded by a complete sentence.

The examples below are <u>not</u> Standard English although you often see similar use.
Incorrect – 1. He asked everyone to: be on time, complete the work, and be conscientious.
Incorrect – 2. Please include:
        a. your address
        b. your phone number
        c. you email address

Colons introducing lists, explanations, quotations, etc. should be preceded by complete sentences.

Other Colon Uses

Notice the common uses of colons below.

Dear Ms. Willis:
Colons follow the salutation of formal letters.

5:30 p.m.
Use colons between hours and minutes.

Genesis 2:11
Use colons between chapters and verses in Biblical citations.

I read an interesting book, *Living Things: An Introduction to Biology.*
Colons may be used between titles and subtitles.

Semicolons

Most Common Function of Semicolons

Analyze the sentences below and see what pattern you can find with the semicolons. What do you notice about the groups of words on each side of the semicolons?
1. I need a new coat; maybe I'll get one for Christmas.
2. He had worked hard; he deserved a raise.
3. Many of my friends have moved away; only a few have stayed.

In all three sentences above, on each side of the semicolon is an independent clause, a group of words with a subject and verb, which could stand alone as a sentence. Unlike a comma, **a semicolon can connect independent clauses without a connecting word.** It may help to think of the semicolon as a period on top of a comma: it has the ability of a comma to connect and the ability of a period to separate complete thoughts.

Some sentences with semicolons do have conjunctive adverbs as below. Notice the additional punctuation, commas, after the conjunctive adverbs *therefore* and *nevertheless* in the sentences below.
1. He studied hard; therefore, his grades improved.
2. I studied a little more than last semester; nevertheless, my grades only slightly improved.

Practice
Analyze the sentences below and correct any errors with semicolons and commas.
1. I have nothing to do today; I am bored to tears.
2. Someone left the door open, consequently, there are flies in the house.
3. Please turn down the stereo, I can't hear your father on the phone.
4. The fire blazed out of control, the rangers, meanwhile, hoped for rain.
5. Do your chores; otherwise, you will get no allowance.
6. We may visit Utah, on the other hand, we may go to Georgia.
7. Thousands signed the petition, accordingly, the bill was defeated.
8. I closed the account, I did, however, open a new one.

Another Semicolon Function

Semicolons have another important use. Analyze the sentences below to determine the pattern.
What would be the problem if all the semicolons in the two sentences below were replaced with commas?
1. I found four kinds of errors in his paper: comma splices; quotation marks, both single and double; possessives, those with apostrophes before the *s*; and fragments.
2. He has a few close friends: Claudia, a piano teacher from Illinois; Quinn, a chef at the best restaurant in town; Aidan, a jazz bass player; and Brett, a historian.

Without semicolons readers might get confused about where one item ends and another begins. This is especially true when one or more items in a series include information about the item.
Semicolons can be used to separate items in a series when commas might be confusing.
Note: Semicolons never introduce a list (a function of colons).

Practice with Semicolons and Commas

Analyze the sentences below and correct any errors with semicolons and commas.
1. I have nothing to do today; I am bored to tears.
2. Someone left the door open, consequently, there are flies in the house.
3. Please turn down the stereo, I can't hear your father on the phone.
4. The fire blazed out of control, the rangers, meanwhile, hoped for rain.
5. Do your chores; otherwise, you will get no allowance.
6. We may visit Utah, on the other hand, we may go to Georgia.
7. Thousands signed the petition, accordingly, the bill was defeated.
8. I closed the account, I did, however, open a new one.

Practice with Semicolons and Colons

Make any necessary corrections in sentences below by using colons or semicolons.
1. My sister has one goal; to get down to 115 pounds.
2. This computer has distinct advantages: more memory, twenty gigabytes, less expensive peripherals, a wide range of software, including data base, word processing, and graphics, and a simplified keyboard..
3. Always walk against traffic, otherwise, you may get hit from behind.
4. Dee had a good idea, have everyone chip in for a gift.
5. Some people live their dreams, some people close their eyes.
6. We have a few things in common, we are, however, very different.
7. She has little time to read, she works twelve hours a day.
8. Remember three things, nothing is free–someone must pay, anything wears out with constant use, especially friends, and things happen beyond our control, so roll with the punches.

Periods

How are periods used in the sentences below?
1. He expects all his students to understand grammar.
2. The letter was addressed to Suzie Queue, M.D., at the hospital.
3. We are meeting with Dr. L. W. Cobb at 3 p.m. today.

Periods are used to indicate the end of sentences and for initials and abbreviations.

Question Marks

Direct Questions

Notice the different forms of sentences in the sentences below and how question marks are used.

> What time is it?
> "What time," she asked, "does the train leave?"
> Did she actually say, "The deadline is long gone"?
> It's already finals week?

In the first sentence above, the question mark follows an obvious question. The second sentence includes a question in a direct quotation, interrupted by the speaker; notice that the question mark comes after the question is completed. In the third sentence, the quotation is not a question; the question is actually outside the quotation, so the question mark is outside the quotation marks. The fourth sentence would not be read as a question without the question mark. These are examples of the most common uses: **Use a question mark at the end of a direct question.**

Other uses of question marks are demonstrated below. What are the patterns?

> You didn't really say that, did you?
> Have you seen your aunt lately? Your uncle? Your cousins?
> An unidentified source – a former employee maybe? – leaked the story.
> A long time ago (ten years?) we met in Singapore.
> She worked six (?) hours overtime.

The first sentence above begins with a statement and concludes with a tag question. The second sentence is a series of questions, with a complete question followed by related, incomplete (elliptical) sentences. The dashes interrupt the main idea of the third sentence to ask a question, similar to the parentheses in the fourth sentence, and the question marks go inside the dashes and parentheses. The question mark in parentheses in the fifth sentence indicates uncertainty about the number. These are all acceptable uses of question marks.

Indirect Questions

Why do you suppose question marks are not used in the sentences below?

> She asked if I had been to Montana.
> My fencing instructor asked me what the maneuver was called.

Neither of the sentences above is a direct question. They are indirect, and **indirect questions do not take question marks.**

Punctuation in the sentences below is <u>not</u> Standard English. Try to determine why.

> Why would she say that??
> Can you believe it?!
> He asked, "Do you have a date for Saturday?".
> "Where did he go?," she asked.

In informal writing, some writers double question marks or combine question marks with exclamation points for emphasis. This is not appropriate for academic or professional writing. In the first sentence above, if you want to emphasize, italicize *Why* or *that*. In the second sentence let the phrasing of the question itself indicate the stress with just a question mark. In the third sentence the question mark is sufficient to end the quotation and sentence; no period is needed. In the fourth sentence the question mark ends the quotation, and the lower case *she* indicates that the sentence continues, so no comma is needed. **Generally, don't double question marks with other punctuation marks.**

An <u>exception</u> to the general rule about not doubling punctuation appears below. Why is it appropriate?

Caught off guard by his comment, she said, "Why would you possibly say . . .?"

An ellipsis followed by a question mark indicates an unfinished question, fairly common in dialogue.

Exclamation Points

What do exclamation points indicate in the following sentences?

"Ouch!" he yelled when he hit his finger with the hammer.

What an amazing sculpture!

Get out!

I can't believe you did that!

Obviously, exclamation points follow exclamations, but notice the different kinds of exclamations. The first sentence contains a one-word exclamation of pain; the second an exclamation of awe; the third an emphatic command; and the fourth a strong statement of disbelief—all strong feelings of some sort, whether in the form of a sentence, fragment, or single word. **Exclamation points indicate strong feeling.**

<u>Misuse of Exclamation Points</u>

Below are examples of exclamation points in informal writing—which may be appropriate for personal notes, informal emails, texting, etc. However, such use is not appropriate for academic, business, legal, and other more formal writing. Why, do you suppose?

It was the craziest thing I'd ever heard!!!

Can you believe it?!

Using more than a single exclamation point to end a sentence is overkill; one does the job. Combining a question mark and an exclamation point is not standard English and is not appropriate for formal writing. (Actually, in 1962 a combination exclamation point/question mark (‽) called the "interrobang" was invented by Martin K. Speckter and was included on some typewriters. The symbol is even available on MS Word today if you select the Wingdings 2 font and type the right bracket] key. This is not to suggest that you use it in formal writing, however.) **Do not overuse exclamation points.** (Notice no exclamation point in that sentence.)

Quotation Marks

Analyze the pairs of sentences below and see what pattern you can find for the use of quotation marks.

1a. She told him to leave the package on the porch.

1b. She said, "Please leave the package on the porch."

2a. The President indicated that the buck stops with him.

2b. The President made one simple statement: "The buck stops here."

3a. The manager said he wanted someone with experience.
3b. The manager demanded, "I want someone with experience."

Notice that quotation marks are used around direct, exact quotations in sentences 1b, 2b, and 3b. The other sentences contain only indirect quotations, which do not require quotation marks. **Use quotation marks for direct quotations.**

Analyze the sentences below to determine other patterns for quotation marks.
1. Robert Frost's poem "The Road Not Taken" is the story of Matt's life.
2. My favorite song in the musical *Cats* is "Memory."
3. The fifth chapter of the book is "Telling Facts."
4. He wrote the article "Too Good to Miss" in the *New York Times*.
5. "Science and Culture" is a thought-provoking essay by Huxley.
6. The first thing my mother used to read in the newspaper is "Dear Abby."
7. She assigned a short story by Eudora Welty, "A Visit of Charity."

Notice that quotation marks are used around short works (unlike books and other titles, which will be considered in the section on italics and underlining). **Titles of short works and sections of longer works – poems, songs, chapters, articles, essays, columns, and short stories – are surrounded with quotation marks.**

Analyze the sentences below to determine another use of quotation marks.
1. Their "democracy" is really a thinly-disguised oligarchy.
2. A timely shove "helped" me into the mud puddle.

The quotation marks in the two sentences above highlight words to show a slightly different meaning from the usual. **Quotation marks are used to designate words with ironic or special meaning.** (Note: It is usually best to avoid quotation marks with slang expressions or clichés. If the expression is appropriate, omit quotation marks; if it isn't appropriate, omit the expression.)

Single Quotation Marks
Analyze the sentences below to determine another use of quotation marks.
1. She teased, "I won't say 'I told you so,' but I did tell you so."
2. Mark said, "I am sure Elton John wrote 'Your Song.' "
Single quotation marks are used for a quotation or title within a quotation. Do not use single quotation marks otherwise. Notice also the use of single and double quotation marks together (' ") when the title ends the quotation in #2 above. Notice also that the quotation marks come <u>after</u> the period.
Note: You may notice in British writing that the use of single and quotation marks is the opposite of American.

Parentheses

What is the purpose of the parentheses ( ) in the following sentences?
Lisa spent a long time (about ten hours straight) writing the paper for English.
Gary spent an equal amount of time (or close to it) playing Tetris.

In each of the sentences above, information that interrupts the flow of thought is set apart in parentheses. This is the most common use of parentheses: **Enclose additional, less important information in parentheses.**

Notice the patterns of parentheses in the sentences below:

My Spanish is limited to *ola* (hello) and my German to *auf wiedersehen* (goodbye).

She works for the FCC (Federal Communications Commission).

Contracts are governed by the Uniform Commercial Code (UCC).

Parentheses are used to enclose translations, spelled out initials of organizations, rules, procedures, diseases, time periods, etc., or initials following the spelled-out organization, rule, etc.

Compare the sentences below. Notice the punctuation.

1. I worked diligently on the project (I can't remember how long exactly) before finally giving up and paying someone else.

2. We spent three weeks (Did I already say that?) in the Adirondacks.

3. All the money was spent before the end of the fiscal year. (That always seems to be the case.) Consequently, the equipment purchase was postponed two months.

In the examples above, the parentheses enclose what might be called an "aside" or comment on the side or editorial comment. In #1 the complete sentence within the parentheses (interrupting the main sentence) is not followed by a period. In #2 the complete sentence in parentheses also interrupts the main sentence but requires a question mark to indicate that it is a question. In #3, the complete sentence within the parentheses is punctuated with a period because it is separate from the sentences before and after it.

When information in parentheses is a complete sentence, do not include an end punctuation mark inside the parentheses unless (1) the enclosed sentence is a question or exclamation, or (2) the enclosed sentence comes between two complete sentences.

Notice the use of parentheses with numbers in the rule above.

Parentheses may be used to enclose numbers in a list.

How are parentheses used below?

"It is also possible to *alter* the learning task in various ways such that each alteration requires different behaviors" (Bloom 66).

Bloom says that alterations may require different behaviors (66).

You may have encountered this use of parentheses for in-text citations in academic papers.

Parentheses may be used to enclose references and or page numbers for in-text citations.

Brackets

How are brackets [ ] used in the sentences below?

1. According to Papert, "Mathematically sophisticated [he means highly skilled] adults use certain metaphors to talk about important learning experiences."

2. Her letter said she would "probably arive [*sic*] at six in the morning."

3. "None of this should be understood as a mere *lack* of knowledge on the part of children," says Seymour Papert (*Mindstorms* [New York: Basic Books, Inc., Publishers, 1980] 41).

In sentence #1 the brackets enclose a comment by the writer included in a quotation. In #2 the comment *sic* is bracketed, indicating that the word preceding it was spelled that way in the original quotation, not by the writer quoting it. In #3 the brackets are used within parentheses because additional parentheses within parentheses would be confusing.

Use brackets to enclose your comments within a quotation or to enclose parenthetical information included within material already enclosed with parentheses.

Practice

In the sentences below, make corrections in the use of parentheses and brackets. This may involve deleting, adding, or changing. Or perhaps a sentence will be correct as is.

a. The only reason she left at least the only one I can imagine was to find herself.

b. The committee made three recommendations: 1 purchase new equipment; 2 upgrade software; 3 hire a systems administrator.

c. If I win the sweepstakes (Get serious!), I plan to tour Europe all summer.

d. In the original version he wrote, "We plan to sine *sic* a new contract in the spring."

e. It was obvious (at least to me (or that's how I remember it) and my brother) that she was out of line.

Slashes

Analyze the following sentences to determine uses of slashes.

> Everyone should bring her/his best work to the art show.
> In rhetoric we studied the either/or fallacy, also called the black/white fallacy.
> Dear Sir/Madame:
> Steven Spielberg was producer/director of *ET*.
> His article is published in the Spring/Summer edition.
> We're looking for the next Denver/Chicago flight.
> Her birthdate was 6/28/2004.
> We went to http://www.apastyle.org/learn/faqs/use-slash-mark.aspx for APA slash rules.
> His hat size is 6 7/8.
> Do not exceed the 60 miles/hour speed limit.

Slashes are used to show options, overlapping, connections, dates, internet addresses, fractions, and substitutes for words like *per* (as in 60 miles per hour). Of course, sometimes hyphens are used for the same purpose.

Note: A common use of slashes to show options is *and*/or, but many style guides (legal writing in particular) frown on using *and/or* because of possible misreading.

Slashes are sometimes used as shortened forms, such as *c/o* for *care of, w/* for *with, w/o* for *without,* and *n/a* for *not applicable.* These may not be acceptable in some writing, such as academic, and be careful about assuming that your readers will know what the slashed initials stand for.

Quoting poetry of fewer than four lines is a slightly different pattern of slashes as shown below:

> The lines "Once upon a midnight dreary / While I pondered weak and weary" are perhaps the most famous in American verse.

Between lines of poetry within text, use a slash with a space on each side.

Practice

Use slashes where appropriate in the following sentences.

1. Dr. Patterson is the provost vice president for the university.

2. He is three-eighths of an inch taller. (Make three-eighths into a numeral.)

3. Every child knows the lines, "Twinkle, twinkle, little star. How I wonder what you are!"
4. If someone calls, tell him her I'll be a few minutes late.

Dashes

First, let's distinguish between dashes and hyphens. What is the difference in the use of the hyphen (between *sixty* and *five*) and the dashes (– or --) in the sentences below?

> The sixty-five rabbits were released in the courtroom.
> He didn't like the answer – an emphatic "no."
> My friend--as he calls himself--borrowed my car and wrecked it.

In the first sentence, the number *sixty-five* is connected by a hyphen. **Hyphens connect.**
In the second sentence, the dash separates the answer from the rest of the sentence. In the third sentence the dashes indicate a parenthetical comment. **Dashes separate but indicate a relationship.** Do not use a hyphen in place of a dash or vice versa. For dashes, use two hyphens together, or your word processor may offer an "em dash" (a long dash that takes the place of two short hyphens).

Let's analyze some sentences to see more specifically how dashes are used.
What does the dash do in the sentence below?

> The company did indeed sign the contract – after the specified date.

The dash is used to emphasize that the contract was signed *after* the specified date.

What do the dashes do in the sentence below?

> Derek stubbed his toe – actually several toes – as he jumped onto the porch.

The dashes separate a restatement.

Why is the dash used in the sentence below?

> To improve his backhand, he worked and worked and worked – and finally gave up.

A dash can indicate a dramatic pause and shift.

Why do dashes in the revised sentence below make it better than the original sentence?

> Original: She bought furniture, chairs, a table, and a hutch for the dining room.
> Revised: She bought furniture – chairs, a table, and a hutch – for the dining room.

In the above revision, dashes separate a series of appositives from the subject, preventing reading *furniture* as part of a list of direct objects (furniture, chairs, a table, and a hutch) if a comma is used instead as in the original sentence. **Dashes can prevent misreading**.

To elaborate a bit on using dashes for emphasis, compare the following sentences.

> She offered some strange advice – something about a long walk off a short pier.
> She offered some strange advice: something about a long walk off a short pier.
> She offered some strange advice, something about a long walk off a short pier.

Any of the three sentences above is grammatically acceptable for setting apart an appositive. The use of the comma is the least emphatic, the colon introduces, and the dash indicates a break for emphasis. As a writer, you can choose whichever works best for your purpose.

Would a colon work after *sayings* in the following sentence?
  Old sayings – aphorisms, adages or axioms – that we trust aren't always valid.

A colon would not work because it wouldn't be preceded by a complete idea, and because the appositives interrupt the main idea. A colon would work if the appositives were at the end of the sentence:
  We can't always trust old sayings: aphorisms, maxims or axioms.

If the same sentence were written with commas instead of dashes (as below) what would be the problem?
  Old sayings, aphorisms, adages or axioms that we trust aren't always valid.

With commas the reader might misread "sayings, aphorisms, adages, or axioms" as a series, a compound subject, instead of reading *sayings* as the subject, followed by a series of appositives renaming the subject.

To sum up dashing possibilities, **dashes can separate for emphasis, restatement, dramatic pauses, or clarity.**

Practice
Use dashes where you think appropriate in the following sentences.
1. Her reasons for the promotion, hard work, time in rank, and service, impressed the committee.
2. He stood by her, or sat by her, as it were, during every minute of the unjust trial.
3. Cassidy, breathless from running, chasing the kitty, and yelling, clutched Grandma's leg and sighed.
4. Everywhere we went, and we covered a lot of ground, we saw incredible scenery.
5. Eventually he said no to her request, *not* the response she was hoping for.
6. David labored with the pictures, mounting slides, organizing materials, and showed up late.

Hyphens

Hyphens in Prefixes

Compare the words below to find hyphen patterns with prefixes. (Incidentally, all the words in both columns are spelled as in a standard dictionary.) Do you see a consistent pattern?

nonprofit	non-believer
nonstop	non-issue
Neoplatonism	neo-Darwinism
neoclassic	neo-Gothic
antibiotic	anti-war
antifreeze	anti-federalist
midlife	
midsize	mid-century

No consistent pattern, is there? **Sometimes prefixes are hyphenated and sometimes not.** Over time, many words that are originally hyphenated lose the hyphen. Unless you are certain of the current spelling of words with prefixes that might be hyphenated, look them up in a dictionary. Let's look at uses for hyphens.

Hyphens in Compound Words

Frequently words like *shoe* and *lace* are paired to form compound words like *shoelace*. What patterns do you see in the following compound words?

fireplug	fire-eater	fire engine
headmaster	head-on	head start
seaman	sea-maid	sea lion
crosscut	cross-eyed	cross fire

Once again, there is no consistent pattern. **Compound words may be combined into a single word or hyphenated or kept separate.** Those connected without hyphens are called "closed compounds"; those with hyphens are, not surprisingly, called "hyphenated compounds." Those like the third group above with spaces and no hyphens are called "open compounds."

Many compound words are familiar, and you probably hyphenate them without a thought. Others are less familiar but may be found in a dictionary. Many compounds, though, are not in the dictionary and come in a variety of patterns. Some patterns are consistent. Analyzing helps you remember them. Examine the numerous patterns below.

Hyphens in Numbers

What pattern do you find in the compounds below?

> thirty-five
> seventy-sixth
> three-sixteenths

These spelled-out numbers or fractions are hyphenated.
Spelled-out numbers *twenty-one* (or *twenty-first*) through *ninety-nine* (or *ninety-ninth*) and spelled-out fractions are hyphenated.
In the sentences below, how are those numbers used (noun, pronoun, adjective...)? What does this suggest about how compounds can be used?

> Thirty-five was a good estimate.
> It was her seventy-sixth birthday.

In sentence a. the compound is a noun, specifically the subject; in sentence b. the compound is an adjective describing *birthday*. Do you suppose that holds true for other compounds? How are the compounds used in the sentences below?

a. Most five-year-olds know the alphabet.
b. My aunt runs marathons, unusual for a sixty-year-old.
c. Their sixteen-year-old daughter got her license.
d. The 653-year-old tree was here when Columbus visited.

In a. and b. the compounds are used as nouns (one as a subject, one as an object of the preposition *for*). **Ages indicated by a number plus *year* and *old* are hyphenated when used as nouns.** In c. and d. the compounds (ages) are used as adjectives. **Ages indicated by a number plus *year* and *old* are hyphenated when used as adjectives preceding and describing a noun or pronoun.**

Staying with the compound ages for a moment, compare c. and d. above with e. and f. below. What happens when the ages used as adjectives come after the noun they describe?

e. Their daughter is sixteen years old.
f. The tree, 653 years old, was here when Columbus visited.

Notice that both ages follow the noun they describe: in e. "fifteen years old" is used as a predicate adjective, and in f. "653 years old" is an adjective phrase. These are called "open compounds."
Ages following a noun or pronoun that they describe (either immediately or after a linking verb) are not hyphenated.

Hyphens in Compound Adjectives

What function do the compounds have in the following sentences?
>   Germany had a <u>short-lived</u> alliance with Russia.
>   Her <u>dog-eared</u> book had been passed down through four generations.

The compound *short-lived* describes the noun *alliance,* and *dog-eared* describes the noun *book,* so both compounds are used as adjectives and are called, appropriately enough, "compound adjectives." Notice what kinds of words (parts of speech, e.g., noun, adverb) are connected with hyphens to form compound adjectives below.

>   <u>Adjective + verb</u>
>   >   strong-smelling
>   >   sweet-tasting
>   <u>Adverb + verb</u>
>   >   half-baked
>   >   even-tempered
>   <u>Adjective + noun</u>
>   >   three-mile
>   >   long-term
>   <u>Noun + verb</u>
>   >   love-starved
>   >   rain-drenched
>   <u>Verb + adverb</u>
>   >   bent-over
>   >   broken-down
>   <u>Prepositional phrase</u>
>   >   off-the-wall
>   >   in-your-face
>   >   over-the-counter
>   <u>Multiple-word phrases</u>
>   >   happy-go-lucky
>   >   devil-may-care
>   >   hard-and-fast
>   >   dog-eat-dog

As you can see, compounds take numerous forms.

An exception to the hyphenated adverb + verb compound is demonstrated in the following sentence:
>   She refused to employ the <u>widely accepted</u> practice of stretching before running.
Adverbs ending in *-ly* are not connected with verbs by hyphens.

Hyphens in Noun Compounds

How are the compounds used in the sentences below?
>His <u>mother-in-law</u> took him into the business.
>The argument mushroomed into a <u>free-for-all</u>.

These compounds are both used as nouns, *mother-in-law* as a subject and *free-for-all* as an object of a preposition. **Hyphens show a combined meaning in noun compounds.**

Hyphens for Clarity

In the sentences below, why do you suppose one word in each pair is hyphenated and the other word is not?
>He works in a <u>co-op</u> with other farmers.
>We built a pigeon <u>coop</u>.

>The <u>re-creation</u> of the crime scene revealed important clues.
>People generally prefer <u>recreation</u> over work.

The words in each pair above are pronounced differently and have different meanings, but without hyphens they could be confused. **Hyphens are sometimes used to avoid confusion between words that may be spelled the same with different meanings and pronunciations.**

Suspended Hyphens

What do you notice about hyphens in the following sentences?
>Nine-, ten-, and eleven-year-old students experience growth spurts.
>The researches gave pre- and post-tests to measure improvement.

To avoid repetition of compounds such "nine-year-old, ten-year-old, and eleven-year-old students" or "pre-tests and post-tests," you may use elliptical compounds with hyphens; that is, use the first word of the compound followed by a hyphen, which will indicate to the reader that the end word(s) in the elliptical compound will complete the final compound.
In a pair or series of compounds with the same basic elements, use a hyphen and space or hyphen and comma when appropriate to indicate an omission.

Hyphens in Random Prefixes and Suffixes

Here are some commonly hyphenated prefixes.
>Her <u>ex-husband</u> had <u>post-traumatic</u> stress from what he called an <u>un-American</u> war.
>The professor gave an <u>all-encompassing</u> talk about <u>self-esteem</u> with <u>pre-adolescents</u>.
(Note: *un-* is hyphenated with capitalized words.)
Here are some commonly hyphenated suffixes.
>We were happy to hear that the <u>governor-elect</u> was serious about a tax cut.
>You may call us at a <u>toll-free</u> number.
>There were probably <u>fifty-odd</u> students at the conference.
>His <u>rapier-like</u> comments offended his subordinates.
>The new director is a <u>production-wise</u> artist.

Refer to newly elected officials by adding the suffix *-elect* with a hyphen to the office.
Other common hyphenated suffixes are *-free*, *-odd*, *-like,* and *-wise.*

Hyphens to Break Words

With word processors automatically scrolling from one line to the next, hyphenating words at the ends of lines has become less common. Yet to justify (make even) margins, writers sometimes hyphenate words. What four patterns of line-ending hyphenation do you see in the pairs below?
How many syllables are in the words below?

Standard	Non-standard
strength	streng-th
heart	he-art

All these words have only one syllable.
Do not hyphenate one-syllable words.

How long are the words below?

Standard	Non-standard
envy	en-vy
copy	co-py
easy	ea-sy

All those words are short.
Do not hyphenate short words.

How many letters are in the first syllable of each word below?

Standard	Non-standard
avoid	a-void
evoke	e-voke
itinerant	i-tinerant
obesity	o-besity

The first syllable of each of these words is one letter.
Do not hyphenate a single letter.

Where do the syllables split? (You may want to check a dictionary when you're unsure.)

Standard	Non-standard
com-plete	comp-lete
per-fect	perf-ect
sen-sitive	sens-itive

Hyphenate between consonants with most multi-syllable words. (See exception below.)

What patterns do you see below with double consonants?

Standard	Non-standard
shal-low	shall-ow
hap-piness	happ-iness
hall-way	hal-lway
full-ness	ful-lness
omit-ted	omit-ed

The natural syllable break in the *shallow* and *happiness* is between the double consonants. In *hallway* and *fullness* the double consonants are part of prefixes, *hall-* and *full-*.
Split double consonants if they are not part of a prefix or a root word.

Practice
Place hyphens where appropriate in the following sentences.
1. All our dogs are half or full blooded border collies.
2. My three year old nephew already knows the alphabet.
3. Be leery of anti-intellectual people.
4. When you reach twenty five, your car insurance goes down.
5. The mayor elect takes office next week.
6. My sister in law is working toward a Ph.D.
7. When I was sixteen years old, my father gave me his five year old Chevy.
8. The bill requires a two thirds majority to pass.

Apostrophes

Possessives with Apostrophes

Singular Possessives

Analyze the underlined words below and determine (1) if they are singular or plural and (2) how the possessive is formed.

> The <u>book's</u> ending is really a surprise.
> This <u>month's</u> meeting will be held in the council room.
> We all piled into <u>Jerry's</u> new car and went to the beach.
> Eric has been writing <u>his</u> papers with <u>his</u> <u>sister's</u> computer.
> <u>Somebody's</u> carelessness cost the company thousands of dollars.
> I don't want to take credit for someone <u>else's</u> work.
> <u>Everybody's</u> favorite movie was a low budget thriller.
> My <u>boss's</u> sense of humor makes him a good leader.
> In March my biology <u>class's</u> field trip will be a hike to the lake.
> <u>Tess's</u> birthday is March 17.
> Everyone was glad to hear of <u>James's</u> success in college.

All the underlined words are singular, and all end with *'s*. Notice that even the last four examples above – *boss, class, Tess,* and *James* – all form their possessives by adding *'s*. **Possessive forms of singular words are almost always formed by adding an apostrophe then an *s* - even when the nonpossessive form of a singular word ends in *s*.**

<u>**Exceptions to singular *'s***</u> – The rare exceptions to this rule are multi-syllable words which already end in *s* and would sound awkward with the addition of another syllable caused by adding *'s*. Examples of this rare exception are ancient names like *Sophocles, Ulysses,* and *Euripides* which form their possessives by adding only an apostrophe: *Sophocles', Ulysses',* and *Euripides'*. Also, the possessive forms of *Jesus* and *Moses* have traditionally been written with only an apostrophe: *Jesus'* and *Moses'*.

Plural Possessives

Now look at the plural words below and see what patterns you find for forming possessives. What is the nonpossessive form of each word?

He bought twenty <u>dollars</u>' worth of groceries.

Her three <u>friends</u>' contributions totaled fifty dollars.

All the <u>books</u>' covers were worn and needing replacement.

Most students look forward to their three <u>months</u>' vacation.

The <u>Smiths</u>' home was vandalized last week.

She really appreciates both her <u>parents</u>' encouragement.

I can't remember the <u>Thomases</u>' address.

Notice that all the plural forms above would end in *s* if they weren't possessive. For example, *dollars* is the plural of *dollar*, *friends* is the plural of *friend*, and *Thomases* is the plural (family) of *Thomas*. **Plural words ending in *s* form their possessive by adding an apostrophe <u>after</u> the *s*.**

How are the plural words below different from those above?

The <u>men's</u> club has an exclusive membership.

Her <u>children's</u> manners were exceptional.

She writes freelance articles for <u>women's</u> magazines.

The two <u>deer's</u> antlers were locked.

The nursery rhyme tells about the three blind <u>mice's</u> woes.

Notice that all these words are plural without *s*: *men* is the plural of *man*; *children* is the plural of *child*; *women* is the plural of *woman*; *deer* is the same in singular or plural; and *mice* is the plural of *mouse*. **Plural words that do not end in *s* form their possessive by adding *'s*.**

Possessives with Compound Words

What pattern do you see with the compound words underlined below?

His <u>mother-in-law's</u> support helped him get the job.

No one questioned the <u>editor-in-chief's</u> decision to cut the story.

Compound words form their possessives by adding *'s* to the last word.

Compare the possessive patterns of the first three sentences below with the next three – all six showing possession by more than one owner.

Oklahoma is one of Rodgers and Hammerstein's best-known musicals.

Every year they produce one of Gilbert and Sullivan's operettas.

First prize went to Dana and Brad's science project.

We read William Faulkner's and F. Scott Fitzgerald's novels.

The greatest applause came after Barbra's and Ray's performances.

I tried to interpret the radio's and television's conflicting reports.

The first three sentences above involve joint ownership; the next three involve separate ownership. **Joint ownership is indicated by adding *'s* to only the last owner; separate ownership is indicated by adding *'s* to each owner.**

Perhaps an easy way to remember possessives is that you always add *'s* except to (a.) personal pronouns and *whose*; (b.) plural words that already end in *s*; and (c.) a few singular forms that would sound awkward by adding *'s*.

Another easy way to determine possessives (except personal pronouns and multi-syllable names) is the following procedure:

Is the word singular?

If yes, add *'s*.

If no, does the plural nonpossessive end in *s*?

If so, add only an apostrophe.

If no, add *'s*.

Practice
Make possessives from the phrases below. (Example: the voice of my sister - my sister's voice)
1. a house belonging to the Thompsons
2. a paper written together by Sharon and David
3. a business belonging to three women
4. music recorded by George Jones
5. wool shorn from four sheep
6. the engine in your car
7. a card from my sister-in-law
8. the arrest of two thieves

Possessives Without Apostrophes

A few words show possession or ownership without apostrophes. Look at them in the sentences below and see what they have in common besides the absence of apostrophes.

Walter sent <u>his</u> suit and <u>mine</u> to the cleaners.

The workers sent <u>their</u> demands to the company president.

<u>Her</u> cold has gotten better this week.

We submitted <u>our</u> proposal two days before the deadline.

She says the book is <u>hers</u>, but it has "City Library" stamped inside.

<u>Your</u> project is much better organized than <u>ours</u>.

<u>My</u> dog wags <u>its</u> tail constantly.

I'm not sure <u>whose</u> lawn looks nicer, <u>yours</u> or <u>theirs</u>.

Did you notice that all the underlined words except *whose* are personal pronouns, forms of *I, we, you, he, she, they,* and *it*? You may recall the discussion of the personal and personal possessive pronouns in an earlier section. As you can see in the sentences above, **the possessive case of the personal pronouns and *whose* do not use apostrophes.**

Most Commonly Misused Possessive Pronouns
The most commonly <u>misused</u> possessive pronoun forms are illustrated in the <u>incorrect</u> sentences below:

Every song in the program has it's own appeal. INCORRECT

Who's car is this? INCORRECT

It's is a contraction for *it is,* and *who's* is a contraction for *who is.*

The two sentences should be written as below:

Every song in the program has its own appeal. CORRECT

Whose car is this? CORRECT

Practice

Now choose the correct form in the sentences below.

1. Is the red car (yours/your's/yours')?
2. (Whose/Who's) book is this?
3. Joy radiated from the (twin's/twins') faces.
4. I am tired of cleaning up your (children's/childrens') messes.
5. We met several couples at the (Davis's/Davises') party.
6. I buy tickets each year for the (Firemen's/Firemens') Benefit.
7. I attended both (Heart/Heart's) and George Benson's concerts.
8. Every dog has (its/it's) day.
9. They put in a good nine (hour's/hours') work.
10. The (puppy's/puppies') obedience earned him a biscuit.
11. The child was startled by the (geese's/geeses') honking.

Apostrophes with Plural Letters and Numbers and Omitted Numbers

Notice the use of apostrophes in the sentences below.

> His two D's dropped his grade point average to the low 70's.
> I wish I still had my '56 Chevy, a real classic.

The apostrophes in *D's* and *70's* indicate plurals. The apostrophe in *'56* indicates an omission of numbers in the year 1956. **Apostrophes may be used to show plurals of letters and numbers and to indicate omitted numbers.**

Apostrophes in Contractions

Analyze the pairs of words below and notice what they have in common.

would not	wouldn't	is not	isn't
should not	shouldn't	are not	aren't
could not	couldn't	did not	didn't
had not	hadn't	does not	doesn't
has not	hasn't	do not	don't
have not	haven't	was not	wasn't
might not	mightn't		

Notice that all the contractions combine two words, a verb and the adverb *not*, replacing the *o* in *not* with an apostrophe. **Contractions combine two words into a single word, replacing one or more letters with an apostrophe.**

There are two variations to this pattern of combining a verb with *not*. How are the contractions below different from those above?

cannot	can't
will not	won't

Can't replaces a single word, and the apostrophe replaces two letters, *n* and *o*. (Incidentally, *cannot* is often misspelled as two words.) *Won't* replaces *ill* with *o,* a real deviation from the usual pattern.

Contractions can be grouped into other patterns. What do the following contractions have in common?

could have	could've
should have	should've
would have	would've
might have	might've
may have	may've

In the above examples, two verbs have been contracted with an apostrophe.

What is the pattern of contractions below?

I am	I'm	he will	he'll
I have	I've	she will	she'll
I will (shall)	I'll	they are	they're
we are	we're	they have	they've
we have	we've	they will	they'll
we will (shall)	we'll	it will	it'll
you are	you're	who are	who're
you have	you've	who will	who'll
you will		you'll	

The contractions above combine pronouns with verbs. The next group of contractions likewise connects personal pronouns with verbs, but what do you notice that is different?

he's	he is, he has
he'd	he had, he would
she's	she is, she has
she'd	she had, she would
you'd	you had, you would
they'd	they had, they would
it's	it is, it has
it'd	it had, it would
who's	who is, who has
who'd	who had, who would

With the contractions above, the only way the reader knows what the apostrophe replaces is from the context, for example:

He's [He is] late for his appointment; he's [he has] not been feeling well.

What kinds of words do the following contractions combine?

here's	here're
there's	there're
there'll	why'd
how'd	where'd

The contractions above combine adverbs with verbs. The contractions made with *here* and *there* are sometimes confused as subject and verb, leading to problems with subject-verb agreement (see that section of this book).

Another sometimes problematic contraction is *let's*. What does it contract, and what problem do you suppose it might present? Compare the two sentences below.

He lets his dog out every morning.

Let's try something new.

In the first sentence, *lets* is a simple verb. *Let's* in the second sentence is a contraction for *let us,* requiring an apostrophe. This contraction is often misspelled *lets*.

Compare the pairs of sentences below to see a potential problem with the italicized words.

John's going to dinner with Erin this evening at the classiest restaurant in Dallas.

John's going to dinner with Erin was a surprise.

The *lion's* roaring because he has a thorn in his paw.

The *lion's* roaring scared my sister.

Contracting nouns or pronouns with *'s*, though common, may cause the reader to initially misread the contraction as a possessive. Consequently, saying *John is* and *the lion is* would be clearer.

Some people object to contractions altogether in academic writing or other writing called "formal." Writers should always be sensitive to their audiences and write accordingly. If your reader objects to contractions, *it'd* be wise not to use them. Interestingly, virtually all American grammar books have a section on contractions (albeit with a caution about use in "formal" writing). If contractions were absolutely unacceptable, why would the books not simply dismiss them as such without elaboration on how they're formed, etc.?

Mechanics

Capitalization

Capital letters (also called <u>upper case</u>) have several uses. How is a capital used below?

> Capitals can indicate the beginning of a new sentence.

The sentence above explains and demonstrates the most common use of capitals: **Capitals begin new sentences.**

What other use of capitals can you find below?

> Karla offered an alternative: Members could do community service in lieu of dues.

The second half of the sentence is a complete idea following a colon. **Capitals may begin independent clauses introduced by a colon.** However, this use of capitals is optional.

How are capitals used in the following sentence?

> The novel *Accordion Crimes* follows an accordion through various owners.
> We subscribe to *Time* magazine.
> I enjoyed watching *Grey's Anatomy.*

Capitals are used in titles of books, magazines, television shows, and other media.

Not all words in titles are capitalized. In the sentences below, what do you notice about which words are capitalized and which words aren't?

> Charlton Heston played Michelangelo in *The Agony and the Ecstasy.*
> I finally waded through the crowd in front of Van Gogh's *Café Terrace at Night.*
> The orchestra played the Brahms symphony *Variations on a Theme by Joseph Haydn.*
> I just read E.B. White's short story, "The Second Tree from the Corner."

Notice that conjunction *and,* the prepositions *at, on, by,* and *from* are not capitalized, nor are the articles *a* and *the* (when not the first word in the title). **Capitalize the first word, the last word, and all important words of titles of literature, music, or works of art.**

How are capitals used below?

> My favorite contemporary author is Carol Shields from Canada.
> The Sierra Club was founded by John Muir, an American icon.
> The teachings of the *Koran* are sacred for Moslems.
> This year, Mother's Day falls on May 14, a Sunday, of course.
> My uncle, a Greek, speaks French and German.

All the capitalized words above are specific names and are called <u>proper nouns.</u> **Capitalize proper nouns, including persons, places, organizations, nationalities, religious groups, holidays, days of the week, months, and languages.**

What do you notice about the differences in capital use in the underlined words below?

> <u>Governor</u> Clancy, the first Republican <u>governor</u> in twenty years, was re-elected.
> My <u>aunt</u> was always called <u>Aunt</u> Cal because Calliope was too long.
> No other <u>professor</u> would affect me like <u>Professor</u> Davies.

Notice in the above sentences that capitals vary with the words *governor, aunt,* and *professor,* depending on whether they are used with or without a name.
Capitalize people's titles when used with their names.

Notice capital use with the underlined words below.
"Please wake me at seven, <u>Mother</u>," he asked, handing his <u>mother</u> an alarm clock.
I don't remember <u>Dad</u> ever saying anything negative. My <u>dad</u> was a saint.
Mother and *Dad* are capitalized when used as a name but not otherwise. **Capitalize family titles (*Mother, Dad,* etc.) if they are used as names.**

How is the capital used with the underlined word below?
God looked upon <u>His</u> creation and said, "It is good."
Pronoun references to God are capitalized.

How are capitals used below?
The FBI investigated the kidnapping.
The Cold War between the U.S. and the U.S.S.R. resulted in nuclear stockpiling.
The sign on my doctor's door read, "I. M. Quack, M.D."
Capitalize initials of organizations, wars, countries, and titles following names.

Compare the use of capitals in the underlined words below.
People in the <u>West</u> have been characterized as less civilized as those in the <u>East</u>.
We traveled <u>west</u> for three hours before recognizing our mistake.
When directions are used as nouns (usually preceded by *the*), they refer to regions rather than directions.
Capitalize directions when they refer to a region, not a direction.

Compare the use of capitals in the underlined words below. When are capitals used and not used with classes?
Her <u>biology</u> class meets at the inhuman hour of 7 a.m.
My <u>Biology II</u> class was much harder than <u>Biology I</u>.
My English class is an hour after my American history class.
Capitalize specific academic course names but not subject areas (unless the subject is a language or another word normally capitalized.

Italics (Underlining)

Italics or Underlining vs. Quotation Marks with Titles

Compare the uses of italics or underlining (either is generally acceptable) and quotation marks below. All these examples employ Standard English. What patterns do you notice?
His favorite movie is *Schindler's List.*
Watching the musical *The Sound of Music,* we sing along with the song "Edelweiss."
Time magazine had an article about gun control, entitled "Who's Pulling the Trigger?"
<u>Hamlet</u> is one of Shakespeare's best-known tragedies.
We watched the re-runs of <u>Cheers</u> together; our favorite episode is "Sam's Night Out."
We listen to *All Things Considered* every day on National Public Radio.
Newspapers such as *The New York Times* are available online.

The first chapter of Donna Tartt's book <u>Goldfinch</u> is "Boy with a Skull."
I just finished reading Thomas Huxley's essay "Science and Culture."
The pamphlet *Becoming Your Best* gives advice on self-actualizing.

Long works, such as movies, musicals, magazines, plays, television and radio programs, newspapers, books, and pamphlets should be underlined or italicized. Exceptions: Do not use italics or underlining for legal documents, e.g., Declaration of Independence, or the Bible or books of the Bible. As noted in the previous section on quotation marks, short works, such as songs, articles, episodes, essays, and chapters of books should be enclosed in quotation marks.

Italics or Underlining for Other Titles

Determine the uses of italics in the following sentences.
    Vincent van Gogh's painting *Starry Night* inspired a song by Don McLean.
    Lindbergh's plane, *The Spirit of St. Louis,* hangs in the Smithsonian.
    The *Titanic* sank in 1912.
As demonstrated above, **use italics for works of art, names of aircraft and ships.**

Other Italicized Words

    George Orwell was the *nom de plume* for Eric Arthur Blair.
    Synonyms for *perspicacious* include *discerning, perceptive, wise,* and *astute.*
    We couldn't tell if it was the letter *l* or the number *1.*

Use italics or underlining for foreign words that are not frequently used in English, words mentioned as words, and numbers or letters mentioned as numbers or letters.

Numbers (Numerical or Spelled Out)

Knowing whether to write numbers as numerals or words is somewhat confusing because not all grammar books agree, and journalism and business generally follow patterns different from grammar books. For example, <u>in journalism, only numbers under ten are spelled out. Likewise, numerals are often preferred in business.</u>

So what is a writer to do? In all writing, consider the audience. When writing for a newspaper, for example, use journalism rules. When writing in business, look at the best models of writing from peers. The patterns discussed below will follow commonly accepted English grammar used in academic and much other writing. Generally, the trend is to accept the simplest, easiest to read presentation.

What do you notice about the pattern of spelled out numbers vs. numerals in the examples below? (Hint: how many words are in the number?)
    Standard English - We saw about fifty people at the exhibition.
    Nonstandard English - We saw about 50 people at the exhibition.
    Standard English - We saw about two hundred people at the exhibition.
    Nonstandard English - We saw about 200 people at the exhibition.
    Standard English - We saw about 250 people at the exhibition.

Nonstandard English - We saw about two hundred fifty people at the exhibition.
Standard English – We saw 3,250 people at the exhibition.
Nonstandard English - We saw three thousand two hundred and fifty people.

Notice that numbers of one or two words are spelled out, and numbers of three or more words are written as numerals. **Generally, spell out simple numbers of one or two words, and use numerals for more numbers of more than two words.** (Again, remember the information at the beginning of this section about journalism and business writing varying sometimes from academic writing.)

One exception in virtually any writing is shown below. What pattern do you notice?
   Standard English - One hundred fifty students failed the exam.
   Nonstandard English - 150 students failed the exam.
Even in journalism and business writing, numbers that begin sentences are spelled out.
Always spell out numbers that begin sentences.

What if the number beginning the sentence is a long one (e.g., Thirty-two thousand, one hundred twenty-five)? Notice how the examples below take care of the problem, adding a word before the number.
   Exactly 32,125 people attended the concert.
   About 32,000 people attended the concert.

What patterns of numerals/words for numbers do you see in the sentences below?
   She was born on March 8, 1980.
   For most of his life, he lived at 712 Archway.
   My appointment is for 6:30 p.m.
   The Lions crushed the Bengals 36-14.
   The study found an average GPA of 3.2.
   According to the survey, 47 percent of the buyers were satisfied.
   The foundation donated $250,000 for the new center.
   The telephone for the Health Department is 405-271-5600.
   My Social Security number is 123-45-6789.
   She was assigned to the 46th Fighter Squadron.

Use numerals for dates, addresses, exact times, athletic scores, decimals, percentages, exact amounts of money, phone numbers, identification numbers, and military units.

What do the examples below suggest about fractions?
   He gave one half to charity and the other half to his heirs.
   At last count, 3/17ths of the control group developed lesions.
Usually spell out simple fractions such a *one half* or *two thirds*, but use numerals for more complex fractions.

What do the examples below suggest about times?
   At three o'clock this afternoon he received the call.
   At about three in the afternoon he received the call.
   At 3:06 p.m. he received the call.
Spell out times that can be expressed as single words.

What do the examples below suggest about numbers in a series? (Hint: notice the number of words required for each number.)

    The final results included 2,390 ayes, 1,226 nays, and 110 abstentions.

    We found two nails, three bolts, and twelve tacks.

    The population included 67 New Yorkers, 125 Georgians, and 14 Texans.

If all numbers in a series are more than two words, use numerals; if all the numbers in a series are one or two words, write the numbers as words; if the numbers are mixed (some more than two words, some not), be consistent within the series with all numerals or all words.

What problem with numbers do you see below and how is it corrected in the sentence following?

    Original - There were twenty five-year-olds in the class.

    Revised - There were 20 five-year-olds in the class.

    Original - We found the score 1-0 101 times in the record books.

    Revised - We found the score 1-0 one hundred and one times in the survey.

Each of the original sentences above could be misread; these are exceptions to the general rule.
Use a combination of numerals and words to avoid confusion with numbers written right next to each other.

Practice

Edit the following sentences for standard use of numbers. Some may be correct.

She can name 43 of the 50 state flowers.

$95 is a lot of money for a pair of shorts, regardless of the brand name.

He scored in the 85th percentile on the SAT.

The tallest student in the class was 6 feet tall.

My father went bonkers when he saw the two hundred fifty-dollar phone bill.

The judges gave her a 7.5 on the uneven parallel bars routine.

We bought ten packages of potato chips, 26 packages of buns, and 120 wieners.

In nineteen forty-five the *Enola Gay* dropped the first atomic bomb on Hiroshima.

The lecture this evening will begin at 7 o'clock.

Ninety-four members signed up for the blood drive.

On his 15th birthday he told his parents they had only 365 chauffeuring days left.

The Eagles edged the Colts fourteen to three.

Ellipsis Marks

How are ellipsis marks (...) used in the following sentences?

    She was gone for ... about five minutes.

    Can I ... that is, *may* I leave the room?

Ellipsis marks (three consecutive periods with spaces between) may be used to indicate a pause or hesitation.

Compare the two sentences below to see how the ellipsis marks are used.

    According to the plan, "To prevent a serious recession, we must stimulate the economy by attracting new industry with all due haste."

    According to the plan, "To prevent a serious recession, we must stimulate the economy ... with all due haste."

Three ellipsis marks are used to indicate an omission of <u>part</u> of a sentence from a quotation.

Compare the two paragraphs below. In the second paragraph, what has been omitted from the first paragraph? Notice the four ellipsis marks in the second paragraph. Why do you suppose four instead of three?

> "Bicycling is an excellent cardiovascular exercise. It is important to maintain the target heart rate for at least thirty minutes, three times a week. Bicycling is especially good for people whose joints are tender because it is a non-impact exercise."

> "Bicycling is an excellent cardiovascular exercise. . . . Bicycling is especially good for people whose joints are tender because it is a non-impact exercise."

Four ellipsis marks indicate an omission of a complete sentence (or more) from a quotation.

Compare the two sets of poetry lines below for the use of ellipsis marks.

> I advocate a semi-revolution.
> The trouble with a total revolution
> (Ask any reputable Rosicrucian)
> Is that it brings the same class up on top.   –Robert Frost

> I advocate a semi-revolution.
> The trouble with a total revolution
> . . . .
> Is that it brings the same class up on top.   –Robert Frost

A full line of ellipsis marks indicates the omission of one line or more of poetry.

Below is a <u>nonstandard</u> use of ellipsis marks:

> He said, ". . . after the weather changes."

Do not use ellipsis marks to begin a quotation.

Caution: Do not use ellipsis marks to misrepresent a writer's meaning by omitting significant information.

Abbreviations, Initialisms, and Acronyms

The words *abbreviations, acronyms,* and *initialisms* are often used interchangeably but may be considered differently. Typically, <u>abbreviations are shortened forms of words</u>, such as Dr. for Doctor. <u>Initialisms are the first letters of words in an organization or title</u>, such as *FBI*. <u>Acronyms are initialisms that can be pronounced as a word</u>, such as *ASAP* or *NASA*. <u>To simplify discussion, we will use the term *abbreviation* to include acronyms and initialisms.</u>

What patterns do you notice in the abbreviations below?

<u>Group A</u>	<u>Group B</u>
Dr. Janice Black	Janice Black, Ph.D.
Capt. Buck Alberts	Jack Willis, Jr.
Ms. Alicia Davis	Lucy Tooth, D.D.S.
Rev. Frank Talk	Frank Talk, DD
Sen. Sandra Jones	Reginald Snooty, Esq.
St. Thomas Aquinas	Rick Lewis, JD

Titles are usually abbreviated before or after proper names (but <u>not before and after</u> the same name, for example Dr. Janice Black, Ph.D.). Note that abbreviations of academic degrees following names may or may not have periods.

What patterns do you notice in the abbreviations below?

AFL-CIO	IRS
AP	NBC
EKG	NFL
FBI	UPI
FDA	USA
IBM	USC
ID	YMCA
IQ	ZIP

Abbreviations are often used for institutions, organizations, corporations, countries, and other words. The trend is to use these all-capital abbreviations without periods, but sometimes periods are used (for example, with *U.S.*). When spoken, all the abbreviations in the group above are spelled out, for example, F-B-I.

What about the abbreviations immediately below? When speaking, do you spell these out?

AIDS

ASAP

NASA

NATO

OPEC

scuba

UNESCO

The abbreviations above, called <u>acronyms,</u> are typically spoken as words, not spelled out. Many abbreviations are used so often that we may not know what they stand for. For example, did you know that *scuba* (which isn't capitalized) stands for self-contained underwater breathing apparatus? The word *acronym* is frequently used to refer to any initialism, but is generally defined as an abbreviation pronounced as a word.

What patterns do you notice in the abbreviations with dates below?

523 B.C.

44 AD

54 B.C.E.

Abbreviations are used with numerals for specific dates: "before Christ" (B.C. or BC), *"anno Domini" (A.D. or AD)*, and "before the common era" (B.C.E. or BCE). These abbreviations may include or omit periods but will always be capitalized.

What patterns do you notice in the initialisms with times below?

6:30 a.m.

9:15 AM

7:45 P.M.

Notice the options above when abbreviations are used with numerals for specific times before noon and after noon. For afternoon, use *a.m.* or *A.M.* or *AM* (abbreviations for Latin *ante meridiem* – before midday), and for after noon use *p.m.* or *P.M.* or *PM* (abbreviations for Latin *post meridiem* – after midday). These may be capitalized or lower case. **When *AM* and *PM* are capitalized, periods are optional; in lower case, periods are standard.**

Notice the patterns below with Latin abbreviations:

      c. or ca. (Latin *circa* = about)

      cf. (Latin *confer* = compare)

      e.g. (Latin *exempli gratia* = for example)

      et al. (Latin *et alii* = and others)

      etc. (Latin *et cetera* = and so forth)

      i.e. (Latin *id est* = that is)

      vs. (Latin *versus* = versus)

Notice that **patterns vary in Latin abbreviations, with a single period following all these Latin abbreviations except *e.g.* and *i.e.***

Incidentally, many writers confuse *e.g.* with *i.e.* Observe their different meanings below.

      Many states (e.g., Michigan, Minnesota, Missouri, Mississippi) begin with *M.*

      My cat is corpulent, i.e., fat.

Use e.g. if you mean "for example," and use i.e., if you mean "that is" or "in other words."

Notice the difference in abbreviations for states in complete addresses (as on envelopes) vs. Standard English in sentences:

      1234 Sunny Lane, Norman, OK 73069

      He has lived in Oklahoma for twenty years.

Spelling out the names of states is standard except with complete addresses.

Our biggest concern as writers should be clarity. Think in terms of Murphy's Law: If something can be misread, it will be. Several things can make writing unclear. Consider the examples below.

Long intrusions

Original

Smith's testimony regarding his injuries and his ability to work or attend retraining classes supports the court's award.

Revised

The court's award is supported by Smith's testimony regarding his injuries and his ability to work or attend retraining classes.

In the original sentence above, notice the long intrusion between the subject *testimony* and the verb *supports*. The revision reads much easier by restructuring with a new subject and verb, "award is supported. The revision is an acceptable use of passive voice. **Generally avoid extended subjects with descriptors that delay the verb.** Long intrusions anywhere in a sentence may be problematic.

Nonparallel elements

Original

The problems arising from unilateral action will be discussed first and then the circumstances under which joint leasing or developing are ordered.

Revised

We will discuss first the problems arising from unilateral action, then the circumstances under which joint leasing or developing are ordered.

The original sentence above leaves the reader hanging, expecting a continuation at the end of the sentence like "will be discussed." **Using parallel structure makes many sentences clearer and easier to read.**

Reader expectation from signals

Original

To parents, dropouts, bikers, and dopers are suspicious characters.

Revised

Dropouts, bikers, and dopers are suspicious characters to parents.

The original sentence may appear at first to begin with a preposition and three objects – to parents and dropouts and bikers and dopers. Readers discover as they read, and signals like *to* and the series of commas can cause readers to expect something different from what the writer intended. Restructuring the sentence eliminates misreading.

Similarly, notice the possible misreading of the original sentence below.

Original

He said he saw a young woman carrying a baby and her husband enter.

Revised

He said he saw a young woman carrying a baby enter with her husband.

In the original sentence above, readers may expect the conjunction *and* to connect the two nouns around it, as if she were carrying a baby and her husband. Again, restructure the sentence to clarify. **Be aware of reader expectation prompted by signals such as punctuation and arrangement of words.**

Punctuation problems

Original
Harry likes everyone in the group but Jeff has only a couple of friends.
Revised
Harry likes everyone in the group, but Jeff has only a couple of friends.

In the original sentence the reader will likely read the sentence wrong (thinking of *but* as *except*). Because it is a compound sentence, standard punctuation of a comma before *but* eliminates the possibility of a misreading.

Similarly, notice the possible misreading of the original sentence below.
Original
Although the police arrested James Smith was the culprit.
Revised
Although the police arrested James, Smith was the culprit.

Again, the omitted comma will cause the reader to see "James Smith" as one name. Inserting the standard comma (following an introductory adverbial clause) remedies the problem. Don't use commas as Band-Aids for structural problems, but **standard use of punctuation can often prevent misreading.**

Combination of problems

Original
Federal laws directed at the control of an evil thought by Congress to require regulation have been upheld.
Revised
Courts have upheld laws directed at controlling evils that Congress believes need regulating.

The original sentence above has a combination of problems. The use of passive voice and a long interruption between the subject *laws* and verb *have been upheld* causes one problem. This is complicated further by a probable misreading of "an evil thought" as *evil* describing *thought* instead of reading *evil* as a noun and *thought by Congress* as a participial phrase describing *evil*. The revision restructures, using active voice to eliminate the long interruption between the subject and verb, and making *evils* an obvious noun to receive the action of *controlling*. **Restructuring sentences can frequently eliminate clarity problems.**

Conciseness

A Baker's Dozen of Fat-cutting Exercises for Verbal Fat

Strategy #1

Compare the pair of sentences below to see what changes are made to eliminate words.

Original

The collateral is adequate enough for Fritz to receive the loan.

Revised

The collateral is adequate for Fritz to receive the loan.

In the revision, *adequate* was removed. Notice what words are removed in the pairs of sentences below and decide why.

Original

To be promoted you will have to meet several necessary requirements.

Revised

To be promoted you will have to meet several requirements.

Original

All employees should return again to the bank promptly after lunch.

Revised

All employees should return to the bank promptly after lunch.

Original

A good loan officer will gather together all the facts before assessing.

Revised

A good loan officer will gather all the facts before assessing.

In the original sentences above, *adequate* and *enough* mean the same thing; *requirements* are always *necessary; return* means to go somewhere *again,* and anything *gathered* is *together*.

In the revisions, the words *necessary, again,* and *together* were removed because they were redundant.

Generally avoid redundant forms. Some redundancies are subtle because they are so common and familiar that we don't notice them. But they are generally unnecessary space fillers.

Practice

Remove the redundancies from the following sentences.

1. The applicant's past history of investments is a major consideration.
2. Regardless of the assets, one problem still persists.
3. He lectured on a variety of different theories of economics.
4. Her desk is always covered all over with papers and folders.
5. One example of Mr. Wilson's architecture, for instance, is the *Wallace Building.*
6. Government and business are both equally responsible for the recession.
7. The contract does not state just exactly what constitutes acceptance.

Strategy #2

Compare the pair of sentences below to see what changes are made to eliminate words.

Original

The original contract called for thirty installments. The original contract was voided.

Revision

The original contract calling for thirty installments was voided.

The repetition of *the original contract* was removed in the revision. What else was changed to combine the two sentences of the original into the single revised sentence?

The form of the verb *called* was changed to the present participle *calling,* thus making *calling for thirty installments* a participial phrase (discussed in the section on Verbals earlier in this book) to describe *contract.*

Examine the sentences below to see the changes – what the revisions eliminate and how the sentences are combined. Hint: the repetition in the original sentences may not be exact, but substitute repetition.

Original

We recommend a $50,000 settlement. This would prevent going to court.

Revision

We recommend a $50,000 settlement to prevent going to court.

Original

Mr. Jones has filed bankruptcy. His action has caused a panic among his creditors.

Revision

Mr. Jones has filed bankruptcy, causing a panic among his creditors.

Original

Averil G. Smith is the owner of the car. Mr. Smith is five months behind in his payments.

Revision

Averil G. Smith, the owner of the car, is five months behind in his payments.

In the first revision, the repetition of *this* (substitute for *settlement*) is removed along with the helping verb *would* and replaced with *to,* forming an infinitive phrase (discussed in the earlier section on Verbals).

In the second revision, the repetition of *His action* (substitute for *bankruptcy*) is removed, along with the helping verb *has,* and the form of the verb *caused* is changed to *causing,* creating a participial phrase describing *bankruptcy.*

In the third revision, the repetition of *Mr. Smith* (substitute for the whole name) is eliminated, along with the verb *is,* creating an appositive (discussed in an earlier section of this book), *the owner of the car.*

Avoid unnecessary repetition, whether exact or substitute, by combining sentences and changing clauses to phrases.

Practice

Remove unnecessary repetition by combining the pairs of sentences below.

1. The agreement was made between the contractor and the architect. It established a completion date of April 1, 1990.
2. Mr. Manley has made a proposal. The proposal would merge the two companies.
3. Ms. Davis has listed two sources of repayment. The sources are cash flow and liquidation of collateral.

4. Dr. Android believes the new equipment will enhance his practice. This will enable him to service a third more patients.

5. We request a loan of $66,000 @ 13.25 fixed. The loan would be payable in 36 monthly installments.

6. The board meeting has been postponed twice. It is scheduled for next Thursday at 3:30 p.m.

Strategy #3

Compare the pair of sentences below to see what changes are made to eliminate words.

Original

It is possible that your calculations are incorrect.

Revision

Your calculations may be incorrect.

The clause *It is possible* is eliminated and the verb is changed from *are* to *may be* to show the possibility. What changes are made in the revision of the sentence below?

Original

It is a well-known fact that he is successful.

Revision

His success is well-known.

Again, a clause, *It is a well-known fact,* has been removed, and the sentence has been restructured into a single clause with *success* as the subject.

Notice similar restructuring changes in the sentences below.

Original

There is an estate sale scheduled Monday.

Revision

An estate sale is scheduled Monday.

Original

There are several clients who want to retain him as their attorney.

Revision

Several clients want to retain him as their attorney.

In the two pairs of sentences above, *there* and other words are removed to simplify. *There* is an adverb most often used to tell <u>where</u> but is never a subject. The actual subject of the original sentence, *sale,* is moved to the beginning. In the second original sentence the subject clients is moved to the beginning, and *There are* and *who* are removed. A good strategy to eliminate *there* is to find the actual subject and reorganize the sentence to begin with the subject.

There and *it* often serve no real function in a sentence and are called "expletives." **Eliminate expletives such as *there* and *it* when their removal makes sentences more concise and readable.**

Practice

Remove unnecessary repetition by combining the pairs of sentences below.

1. There is cause for concern by the bank regarding the liquidation of his assets.
2. It is certain that the company will default on its loans.
3. There are thirty cases that involve similar circumstances.
4. In the application there are three major sources of income listed.

5. If the court reverses the decision, it will result in a rash of appeals in similar cases.
6. There is a possibility that the auditors will suggest a procedural change.

Strategy #4

Compare the pair of sentences below to see what changes are made to eliminate words. Begin by determining if the subject of each sentence is doing the action or receiving the action.

Original

The ball was hit by Bob.

Revised

Bob hit the ball.

In the original sentence, the subject *ball* is receiving the action. In the revised sentence, the subject *Bob* is doing the action. Notice that the revised sentence is more concise and more direct. Analyze the sentences below and see if the patterns are similar.

Original

A decision was made by the manufacturer to recall the batch of defective parts.

Revised

The manufacturer decided to recall the batch of defective parts.

In the original sentence, the subject *decision* receives the action, and in the revised sentence, the subject *manufacturer* does the action. As discussed in an earlier section, a subject doing the action is active voice; a subject receiving the action is passive voice.

Let's examine one more example of the change from passive to active, and then look for another similarity among all the pairs.

Original

A credit life policy was provided by Heartless Insurance.

Revised

Heartless Insurance provided a credit life policy.

Again, the original subject *policy* is passive, and the revised sentence's subject *Heartless Insurance* is active. In all three of the original sentences, the doer is the object of a prepositional phrase beginning with *by*. Reconstructing the sentences means moving that doer into the subject position and making the original subject a direct object after the verb.

Active voice is generally more direct and concise than passive. Passive voice may occasionally be preferred for a different emphasis, for flow between sentences, or for an anonymous doer, all of which are discussed in other sections of this book.

Practice

Restructure the sentences below to convert them from passive to active voice.

1. Based on Fullmore's past performance, approval is recommended by the committee.
2. Her will was rewritten by her attorney after the stock market crash.
3. All the homes have been sold by the firm before the completion of the loan.
4. The next quarterly principal payment will be decreased by extra prepayments.
5. Davis was chosen by over half the delegates to the convention.

Strategy #5

Compare the pair of sentences below to see what changes are made to eliminate words.

Original

The president has a tendency to ramble in his memos.

Revised

The president tends to ramble in his memos.

The revision uses a simple verb *tends* instead of the common but wordy expression *has a tendency.* Such expressions result from changing a verb to a noun (e.g., *tends* to *tendency*) and adding a new verb. Notice the similar patterns in the following pairs of sentences.

Original

We made a decision to pursue the merger.

Revised

We decided to pursue the merger.

Original

You have the freedom to choose.

Revised

You are free to choose.

Original

Everyone on the team with the exception of Lance favored longer workouts.

Revised

Everyone on the team except Lance favored longer workouts.

In the above pairs, words are eliminated by changing the noun *decision* to the verb *decided,* the noun *freedom* to the adjective *free,* and the noun *exception* to the preposition *except.* The noun forms are called *nominalizations,* and we hear, read, and use them often. **Often you can avoid using nominalizations.**

Practice

Restructure the sentences below by eliminating nominalizations.

1. Everyone in the office should be in attendance at the meeting.
2. Please make an adjustment in your schedule for next month.
3. He had some inconsistencies in his testimony.
4. Please let me know if I may be of help to you.
5. The FBI conducted an investigation of his numerous trips to Switzerland.
6. The committee came to the conclusion that the policy should be changed.

Strategy #6

Compare the pairs of sentences below to see what changes are made to eliminate words.

Original

The court did not allow recovery to avoid expanding coverage.

Revised

The court denied recovery to avoid expanding coverage.

Original
The appellate court does not reverse very often.
Revised
The appellate court rarely reverses.

Original
The company gave no consideration to the new code.
Revised
The company ignored the new code.

Original
The contract does not provide for employees not on the payroll as of May 1, 1995.
Revised
The contract provides only for employees on the payroll as of May 1, 1995.

In all the pairs above, *not* or *no* is removed, along with other changes. In the first pair, an antonym replaces the original verb: *denied* instead of *did allow.* In the second pair, the adjective *rarely* replaces *very often,* and the verb form is changed. In the third pair, the verb *ignored* replaces four words.. In the fourth pair, *only* serves the same function as the replaced *nots.*

Often eliminate *not* and *no*, rephrasing with antonyms and restructuring. (Note: You may occasionally wish to sound less forceful and use *not; e.g.,* an attorney representing a company might say "The company did not consider the new code" because it doesn't sound as harsh as "The company ignored the new code.")

Practice
Rephrase the sentences below to *not* and *no*.
1. My brother did not remember his appointment.
2. The defendant did not take care of his duties.
3. His objections to the motion are not important.
4. This provision does not apply to students who are not residents of the state.
5. The firm did not have sufficient funding for the acquisition.
6. We have no objection to the assessment of the property.
7. The will did not mention the children.

Strategy #7
Compare all four pairs of sentences below to see what changes are made to eliminate words. Hint: Notice the verbs.
Original
The speaker's presentation was inspirational to us.
Revised
The speaker's presentation inspired us.

Original
We were unaware she could be so assertive.
Revised
Her assertiveness surprised us.

Original
The Cowboys were the winners over the Giants, 45-6.
Revised
The Cowboys crushed the Giants, 45-6.

Original
In the room was an ugly table that was the most dominating feature.
Revised
An ugly table dominated the room.

In all four original sentences, the verbs are <u>being</u> verbs: *was, were, could be, were, was, and was.* In the revisions, the sentences are restructured using action verbs: *inspired, surprised, crushed,* and *dominated.*

In sentences intended merely to describe and name, *being* verbs (often used as linking verbs) are probably sufficient, but they may rob writing of vitality. **Sentences can often be activated and condensed by looking for good action verbs and rewriting the sentences.**

This may involve changing a verb and adjective, as in the first example above, or it may involve significant restructuring as in the other examples--maybe even selecting a new subject or reducing two clauses to one.

Practice
Restructure the sentences below to replace <u>being</u> verbs with <u>action</u> verbs.
1. Someday you'll be sorry for your procrastination.
2. Tatum was highly desirous of a mocha almond fudge sundae.
3. It was a real disappointment to Carla that her ACT scores were average.
4. He became unconscious in the merciless heat.
5. Everyone in the class is afraid of the final exam.
6. Dave's first three years after high school were unproductive.

Strategy #8
Compare all four pairs below to see what is removed in revision.
Original
The court ordered the company to cease and desist operating the web site.
Revised
The court ordered the company to cease operating the web site.

Original
Each and every person in this room will eventually have to manage a crisis.
Revised
Every person in this room will eventually have to manage a crisis.

Original
Please give a full and complete description of the car.
Revised
Please give a complete description of the car. (*or* Please describe the car completely.)

Original

We noticed that various and sundry items had been removed from the room.

Revised

We noticed that various items had been removed from the room.

Each original sentence above contains a redundant pair of words – *cease and desist, each and every, full and complete.* **Though commonly used, eliminate one of the unnecessary words in redundant pairs.**

Practice

1. Remove the unnecessary words in the sentences below.
2. The undersigned surrenders any and all rights to the property.
3. Is this a true and accurate account of the proceedings?
4. He was accused of aiding and abetting the fugitive.
5. His address ended with a wish that his classmates would fulfill their hopes and desires.
6. First and foremost, we should strive for justice.
7. The best candidate will have honesty and integrity.
8. Both parties will meet to try and find a fair and equitable solution.

Strategy #9

Compare all four pairs below to see what is removed in revision.

Original

A majority of the reasons she offered were legitimate.

Revised

Most of the reasons she offered were legitimate.

Original

New interest rates will be established in the near future.

Revised

New interest rates will be established soon.

Original

In the event that you miss three consecutive payments, we will foreclose.

Revised

If you miss three consecutive payments, we will foreclose.

Original

Subsequent to the Watergate break-in, several White House figures lost their positions.

Revised

After the Watergate break-in, several White House figures lost their positions.

In the sentence revisions above, *most* replaces *a majority of; soon* replaces *in the near future; if* replaces *in the event that;* and *after* replaces *subsequent to.* **Phrases can often be replaced by single words that mean the same thing.**

Practice

Replace the unnecessary phrases with single words in the sentences below.

1. Notwithstanding the fact that our assets are the highest ever, we can't be content.
2. Due to the fact that few people voted, the bond issue failed.

3. Because the defendant acted in a negligent manner, the plaintiff was injured.
4. The new policy stipulates that an audit will be conducted on a regular basis.
5. We don't wish to change companies at this time.
6. The president will in all likelihood appoint a new director.
7. We had a large number of phone calls complaining about the service.
8. She was unable to stay awake in the course of the meeting.

Strategy #10

Compare all four pairs below to see what is removed in revision.

Original - He went quickly across the room.
Revised - He hurried across the room.

Original - Melanie asked in earnest for the money.
Revised - Melanie pleaded for the money.

Original - The board responded negatively to the request.
Revised - The board refused the request.

Original - The dog ate the food quickly and ravenously.
Revised - The dog devoured the food.

In each of the sentence revisions above, a specific verb replaces a less specific verb and adverb: *hurried* replaces *went quickly; pleaded* replaces *asked in earnest; refused* replaces *responded negatively;* and *devoured* replaces *ate quickly and ravenously.* **Specific verbs are often better than unspecific verbs with adverbs.**

Practice
Use specific verbs in the sentences below to replace weaker verbs and adverbs.
1. His daughter looked at him angrily.
2. The pitcher threw the ball hard.
3. Her boss carefully looked over the document before signing.
4. Amber worked hard on the project for weeks.
5. The dancers moved lightly across the floor.
6. His brother, a bodybuilder, walked proudly onto the stage.
7. This organism lives successfully in a warm environment.

Strategy #11

Compare the pairs of sentences below to see what changes are made to eliminate words.

Original - Most of the suggestions she offered were reasonable.
Revised - Most of her suggestions were reasonable.

Original - The books belonging to Mr. Ivory vanished.
Revised - Mr. Ivory's books vanished.

Notice in the first revision that the clause *she offered* is replaced by the possessive *her,* and in the second revision the participial phrase *belonging to Mr. Ivory* is replaced by the possessive *Mr. Ivory's.* **Possessives can often be used instead of phrases and clauses to describe**.

Practice
Change clauses and phrases to possessives in the sentences below.
1. The presentation that Dr. Cross made inspired everyone.
2. He hasn't returned any of the phone calls I made.
3. Few people have heeded the warnings that scientists have given about global warming.
4. The priceless vase owned by the Smiths was stolen.

Strategy #12
Compare the pairs of sentences below to see what changes eliminate unnecessary words.
Original - He pointed to the book that was lying open on the counter.
Revised - He pointed to the book lying open on the counter.

Original - The woman, who was distraught from her loss, hired a lawyer.
Revised - The woman, distraught from her loss, hired a lawyer.

Original – The police found the money, which was stolen.
Revised – The police found the stolen money.

Notice that an adjective clause in each original sentence has been changed to a shorter phrase or a single adjective: *that was lying open on the counter* becomes the participial phrase *lying open on the counter; who was distraught from her loss* becomes the adjective cluster *distraught from her loss;* and *which was stolen* becomes the simple adjective *stolen.* (See earlier sections of this book on clauses, participial phrases, and adjective clusters.) **Descriptive clauses with relative pronouns (*that, which*, who) can often be shortened into phrases or simple adjectives.**

Practice
Reduce clauses to phrases or simple adjectives in the sentences below.
1. The biggest obstacle that was encountered by the task force was apathy.
2. The assailant, who was believed to be a dwarf, absconded with the stilts.
3. The only explanation that was plausible was a short.
4. His paintings, which were only a small part of the collection, sold for millions.

Strategy #13
Compare the pairs of sentences below to see what changes eliminate unnecessary words.
Original - In my opinion, the new program will increase revenue.
Revised - The new program could increase revenue.

Original - A different point of view, I think, will improve the readability.
Revised - A different point of view might improve the readability.

Original – It seems to me that her discussion with Mr. Johnson changed her point of view.
Revised – Her discussion with Mr. Johnson probably changed her point view.

We often use phrases or clauses with first person (*my, I* and *me*) to hedge or avoid sounding definite. In the revisions above, *will increase* becomes *could increase* to eliminate the prepositional phrase *in my opinion; will improve* becomes *might improve* to eliminate the clause *I think;* and the adverb *probably* is inserted, eliminating the hedge *It seems to me.* **Instead of first person (*I, me, my*) clauses and phrases, use less definite helping verbs like *could, might, may,* or *should* or use adverbs *probably* or *likely.***

Practice
Eliminate first person phrases and clauses by adding *probably* and *likely* or by using less definite helping verbs like *might, may, could,* or *should.*
1. I'm pretty sure that the economy will recover with lower interest rates.
2. As the 21st Century unfolds, I think violence in schools will increase.
3. I feel that the activity didn't work because the students needed more practice beforehand.
4. The Yankees will win the pennant this year in my opinion.

Emphasis

When speaking, we emphasize words by speaking louder and with a higher pitch. Consider the possible vocal stresses of the following sentence: Alan broke his leg yesterday.

> ALAN broke his leg yesterday.
> Alan broke his LEG yesterday.
> Alan broke his leg YESTERDAY.

Volume and pitch are not options in writing, so all-capitals, italics, and underlining are common for emphasis. Let's look at several other options.

It-cleft

> It was Alan who broke his right leg yesterday
> It was his leg that Alan broke yesterday.
> It was yesterday that Alan broke his leg.

Although *it* can frequently be avoided for conciseness (see the Conciseness section of this book), it does put emphasis on the word that renames *it* (the predicate nominative) – *Alan, leg,* and *yesterday.*

What-cleft

> What Alan broke yesterday was his leg.

Almost like a question "What?" that ends with an answer, or like a drumroll – bu-bu-bu-boom! *Leg* gets emphasis.

Adverb position

> Yesterday Alan broke his leg.

Typically the first and last words of a sentence get most emphasis, so the adverb *yesterday* may get more emphasis at the beginning of the sentence.

Passive voice

> Alan's leg was broken yesterday.

Although active voice (with a subject doing) is often more direct and concise, passive voice (subject receiving action) can be used to emphasize the final word in a sentence.

Arrange from Lesser to Greater

> He is a murderer, a liar, and a thief.
> He is a liar, a thief, and a murderer.

This is another example of emphasis at the end of a sentence.

Interruptions with Commas

> Teaching is very much like writing.
> Teaching, of course, is very much like writing.

Interruptions typically throw emphasis back on the word preceding them.

Modifiers

> She lectured on the benefits of exercise.
> She lectured convincingly on the benefits of exercise.
> She lectured on the undeniable benefits of exercise.

Modifiers (descriptive words) can put emphasis on the words they describe, as *convincingly* does with *lectured,* and *undeniable* does with *benefits.*

Correlative conjunctions

Teachers and administrators should examine the limits of the classroom.

Both teachers and administrators should examine the limits of the classroom.

Not only teachers but administrators as well should examine the limits of the classroom.

Correlatives (two-part conjunctions) like *both/and* and *not only/but,* emphasize the words they connect.

Inverted sentences

Never before had she encountered such an inconsiderate person.

Intelligence he had in abundance; wisdom, he sorely lacked.

Brothers and sisters have I none; but this man's father is my father's son.

Instead of beginning a sentence with the subject (e.g., She had never before encountered such an inconsiderate person), inverting it puts emphasis on what precedes the subject (*Never* in the first inverted sentence above).

Exclamations

He had a crazy idea.

What a crazy idea he had!

Exclamations obviously emphasize, often because they are inverted sentences.

Action Verbs

Her position on taxes was surprising to us.

Her position on taxes surprised us.

Action verbs emphasize and make sentences livelier.

Transition Position

The defendant shot her husband, but it was in self-defense.

Although the defendant shot her husband, it was in self-defense.

Beginning the sentence with the conjunction *although* emphasizes immediately that a condition will follow in the second half of the sentence, whereas the transition *but* indicates guilt before indicating a condition.

Cumulative Sentences for Fluency, Style, and Detail

The cumulative sentence is a useful tool for all kinds of writing. Used often by literary writers but useful in any writing, cumulative sentences typically employ four kinds of phrases, which we will examine individually.

Cumulative Sentences with Participial Phrases

Notice the flow of the two sentences below:

> The trail moved up the dry shale hillside, avoiding rocks, dropping under clefts, climbing in and out of the old water scars. --John Steinbeck

> The cub saw his mother, crouching down till her belly touched the ground, whimpering, wagging her tail, making peace signs. --Jack London

Analyze the sentences above and look for patterns. For example, could everything after the first comma be left off? If so, why is that information there? What do the phrases such as *avoiding rocks* and *dropping under clefts* describe? What kind of word begins each phrase?

The first part of each sentence ("The trail moved up the dry shale hillside" and "The cub saw his mother") is a complete idea, and the additional phrases add details considered important by the writer. Notice that each phrase begins with a verb (*avoiding, dropping, climbing,* etc.), but each phrase is used as an adjective to describe a noun in the first part of the sentence: *trail* in the first sentence and *mother* in the second. **These participial phrases (verb phrases used as adjectives, discussed in an earlier section on verbals) help the reader see specifically what the writer has in mind. The sentences are called "cumulative" because they accumulate detail.**

Notice that both these sentences by Steinbeck and London are simple sentences (with a single clause, not two or more clauses as in complex or compound sentences), followed by participial phrases describing a noun in the clause. Notice also how they flow and are easy to read. The cumulative sentence is a structure much like a paragraph: a main idea followed by description, like a topic sentence expanded by other sentences.

You may have noticed that all the phrases in the sample sentences above begin with *–ing* verbs (present participle). Notice the different participle forms in the sentences below:

    1. She stood for several minutes, <u>fascinated</u> by the crowd, <u>amused</u> by the clown's antics, <u>amazed</u> at his dexterity.

    2. He picked up the branches, <u>frozen</u> with icicles, <u>broken</u> by the additional weight, <u>strewn</u> around the garden.

The phrases in the sentences above begin with past participles, which may end in *-ed* (as in the first sentence) or may be irregular verbs with different endings, like *broken* and *strewn* in the second sentence.

Why do some phrases begin with present participles (*-ing*) and others with past participles?

Notice that the action in the past participles is <u>done to</u> the word being described (e.g., *She* in the first sentence is <u>being</u> *fascinated* and *amused*, and *branches* in the second sentence are *frozen* and *broken,* not doing the freezing or breaking). In the earlier sentences with present participles, the word being described is <u>doing</u> the action (the *trail* is *avoiding* and *dropping,* and the *mother* is *crouching* and *whimpering*).

Cumulative sentences are useful in any kind of writing, not just literary. Look at the sentences below, examples of persuasive and expository writing.

     1. Mr. Smith is a responsible father, spending a lot of time with his children, providing for all their needs, determined to be the best parent possible, known to neighborhood kids as Papa.

     2. The cumulative sentence is a great vehicle for detail, moving from general to specific, providing continuity, condensing several ideas into a single sentence, used by many authors.

Notice that each of the two sentences above includes present and past participles. Mixing them is fine.

Cumulative sentences may add participles or participial phrases to describe a noun or pronoun earlier in the sentence.

Practice the pattern by adding two or more participial phrases to each of the sentences below. Picture the sentence in your mind, and then describe the person, moon, car, or teacher with actions (e.g., He was a big man, dwarfing his peers, intimidating his foes).

     He was a big man.
     She hurried across the room.
     The moon rose.
     The car crashed into the pole.
     The teacher smiled.

Cumulative Sentences with Adjective Series or Adjective Phrases

The beginning of the discussion of cumulative sentences indicated four kinds of phrases; the first phrases discussed were participles. To begin considering a second kind of phrase, look at the sentence below. What kinds of words follow the dash (*dear, inescapable,* etc.)?

     Thus she passed from generation to generation—dear, inescapable, impervious, tranquil, and perverse.   --William Faulkner

In Faulkner's sentence *she* is described by a series of adjectives: *dear, inescapable, impervious, tranquil,* and *perverse.*

Now notice in the sentences below how adjectives can be expanded into phrases.

     Don Antonio was a large man, heavy, full at the belt, a trifle bald, and very slow of speech.
     --Willa Cather

     They loved to tell stories, romantic and poetic, or comic with a romantic humor.
     --Katherine Anne Porter

Notice in the first sentence Willa Cather describes *man* first with a single descriptive adjective, *heavy,* followed by three phrases also describing *man*. What is the main word in each of those phrases? What are the rest of the words in each phrase doing?

In the Cather sentence, the main words are *full* in the first phrase, *bald* in the second phrase, and *slow* in the third. *Full* is described by "at the belt," *bald* is described by "*a trifle*," and *slow* is described by "of speech." So the main word in each phrase is an adjective, described by other words or phrases ("at the belt" and "of speech" are prepositional phrases).

In the Porter sentence, the phrases "full at the belt," "a trifle bald," and "very slow of speech" are called <u>adjective phrases</u> or <u>adjective clusters</u>. Notice the placement of these adjective phrases. When you think about adjectives, where are they more often located in relation to the word they describe, such as "The quick, brown fox jumps over the lazy dog"?

Adjectives in English are most frequently located in front of the word they describe. But placing a series of adjective phrases in front of the word they describe (*man*) would <u>not</u> work: Don Antonio was a large, heavy, full at the belt, a trifle bald, and very slow of speech <u>man</u>.

So adding adjective phrases after the word they describe allows writers to give more detail. Again, these phrases are useful in all kinds of writing, not just literary.

Notice the examples below with adjectives series and adjective phrases. The first could be in a letter of reference, the second in a grammar book.

> Ms. Williams is an excellent worker, conscientious, punctual, articulate, amiable with everyone, yet willing to voice her opinion.

> As you can see, the cumulative sentence is a great structure—efficient, easy to read, not difficult to write.

Cumulative sentences may add a series of adjectives or adjective phrases to describe a noun or pronoun earlier in the sentence.

Now practice adding adjective series and adjective phrases to the same sentences you expanded earlier with participial phrases. Again, picture the sentence in your mind, and then describe the person, room, moon, car or pole (e.g., He was a big man, tall, muscular in the chest, strong as onions).
> He was a big man.
> She hurried across the room.
> The moon rose.
> The car crashed into the pole.
> The teacher smiled.

Cumulative Sentences with Appositives

The third kind of phrase to consider for cumulative sentences is shown below.

> They will enjoy nothing but the bleakest of New England scenery—a few hardbitten pastures, a rocky wall, a moth-eaten hill, and a stern and pointless old house.   –D.C. Peattie

> The lighter's flame lighted up his features for an instant, the packed rosy jowl, the graying temple, the bulging, blue, glazed eye. – Kay Boyle

What is the main word in the phrase "a few hardbitten pastures"? What is the main word in the phrase "a rocky wall"?

Pastures is the main word in the first phrase, described by "a few hardbitten," and *wall* is the main word in the second phrase, described by "a rocky." What kind of words (part of speech) are *pastures* and *wall*?

They are nouns, which name things. To what word in the first part of the sentence are *pastures* and *wall* referring, and what part of speech is that word?

They refer to *scenery,* another noun. So the phrases "a few hardbitten pastures" and "a rocky wall" (as well as the other phrases in the sentence) are naming *scenery*. We say that these phrases are <u>renaming</u> *scenery* since it has already been named, and as noted in an earlier section of this book, words or phrases that rename are called <u>appositives</u>.

As noted with previous types of phrases in cumulative sentences, appositives are useful in other forms of writing besides literary. Below is an example of expository writing:

The cumulative sentence is invaluable: a powerful tool for enlivening writing, a device used by many professional writers, perhaps the most effective sentence structure for incorporating a lot of detail.

Notice in the sentence above that the appositive phrases containing *tool, device,* and *structure* all rename *sentence*.

Cumulative sentences may add appositives to rename a noun or pronoun earlier in the sentence.

Now practice adding appositives to the same sentences you expanded earlier with different phrases. Again, picture the sentence in your mind, and then rename the person, room, moon, car or pole (e.g., He was a big man, a giant among his peers, a knight without armor, a gentle soul).

> He was a big man.
> She hurried across the room.
> The moon rose.
> The car crashed into the pole.
> The teacher smiled.

Cumulative Sentences with Absolutes
The fourth kind of phrase to consider for cumulative sentences is shown below.

> Mrs. Koch knitted without looking, a fine sweat cooling her brow, her eyes absently retaining a look of gentle attention. – Nadine Gordimer

> After that we rode on in silence, the traces creaking, the hoofs of the horses clumping steadily in the soft sand, the grasshoppers shrilling from the fields and the cicadas from the trees overhead. – E.W. Teale

Does the phrase "a fine sweat cooling her brow" contain a subject and a verb? Could the phrase stand by itself as a sentence? If not, what word would you need to change to make it a complete sentence?

The phrase does have a subject (*sweat*) and a verb (*cooling*) and could be made into a complete sentence (independent clause) by changing the verb to *cooled* or *was cooling*. But Gordimer didn't want it to be a separate sentence, so using the verb *cooling* makes the phrase an absolute, dependent on the first part of the sentence. The same is true with the second phrase, "her eyes absently retaining a look of gentle attention," which could be a separate sentence by changing *retaining* to *retained* or *were retaining*. As is, Gordimer's sentence with dependent phrases flows better than changing the phrases to sentences.

This kind of phrase, as noted in an earlier section of this book, is called an absolute (or nominative absolute), which is a phrase usually containing a subject and verb, made dependent by the form of the verb. In the Gordimer sentence above, the absolutes describe Mrs. Koch and act as adjectives. In the Teale sentence, however, the absolutes don't describe a particular word but instead describe the situation. So absolutes differ from participial phrases, adjective phrases/clusters, and appositives in this regard, sometimes not referring to a particular word.

One variation of the absolute is demonstrated in the sentence below. Can you find the difference between the absolutes below and absolutes discussed above?

> She stood before the crowd, her skin clammy, her face red with embarrassment, her heartbeat off the charts.

Notice that the three absolutes in the above sentence have no verbs. However, the verbs are understood, (e.g., her skin *being* clammy) like the understood *you* in a command.

Absolutes are most often found in literary writing, but they may also be used in expository or persuasive writing, as in the following sentence:

The cumulative sentence is generative, its structure prompting images and details, its rhythm evoking graceful phrasing.

Cumulative sentences may add absolutes to describe something earlier in the sentence.

Now practice adding absolutes to the same sentences you expanded earlier with different phrases and. Again, picture the sentence in your mind, and then add descriptive absolute phrases (e.g., He was a big man, his stature unequaled in his family, his presence intimidating foes on the basketball court).

> He was a big man.
> She hurried across the room.
> The moon rose.
> The car crashed into the pole.
> The teacher smiled.

Cumulative Sentences with Mixed Phrases

So far we have examined cumulative sentences with what is called <u>parallel structure</u> (discussed in an earlier section of this book), some sentences with only participial phrases, some with only adjective phrases, some with only appositives, and some with only absolutes. This was done to isolate and identify the different types of phrases. Notice how phrases in the cumulative sentence below are not parallel.

We watched the movie, an old spaghetti western, starring John Wayne, macho as always, his heroism unparalleled.

Is nonparallel structure okay? Yes, although parallel structure is often important, cumulative sentences like the one above may have more than one type of phrase. Can you identify the four types of phrases in that sentence?

First is an appositive, "an old spaghetti western," followed by a participial phrase, "starring John Wayne," followed by an adjective cluster, "macho as always," and finishing with an absolute, "his heroism unparalleled."

Below is a cumulative sentence with several nonparallel phrases. Can you identify them?
>The deserted farm was a dismal scene, rickety, old and rotting, occupying space but serving no purpose, an eyesore to most, but to a few a sign of peaceful surrender, a sort of white flag.

An adjective series, "rickety, old and rotting," is followed by two participial phrases, "occupying space but serving no purpose," which are followed by an appositive, "an eyesore to most," and then (after the interruption "but to a few") two more appositives – "a sign of peaceful surrender" and "a sort of white flag."

Cumulative sentences may add more than one kind of phrase to describe something earlier in the sentence.

Now practice writing cumulative sentences with different types of phrases in each, expanding the sentences below or composing your own from scratch.

>He was a big man.
>She hurried across the room.
>The moon rose.
>The car crashed into the pole.
>The teacher smiled.
>We listened to the concert.
>He was awed by the abbey.

Index

Abbreviations, 124

Absolutes, 57

Acronyms, 126

Active voice, 22

Adjectives, 10

Adjective clauses, 46

Adverbs, 26

Adverb clauses, 47

Apostrophes, 113

Appositives, 56

Brackets, 105

Capitalization, 119

Clarity problems, 127

Colons, 99

Comma splices, 66

Commands, 41

Commas, 90

    with compound sentences, 90

    with introductory adverb clauses, 91

    with introductory phrases, 91

    with series, 94

    with appositives, 95

    with nonessential clauses, 95

    with dates and addresses, 96

    with introductory expressions, 96

    with transition words, 96

    with direct addresses, 96

    with contrasting phrases, 97

    with tag questions, 97

    with omissions, 97

    with names and titles, 98

    with parenthetical comments, 98

    with direct quotations, 98

Complex sentences, 46

Compounds, 43

Compound phrases, 43

Compound sentences, 45

Compounds sentence parts, 43

Conciseness strategies, 129

Conjunctions, 28

Conjunctive adverbs, 34

Contractions, 117

Contrasting phrases, 99

Cumulative sentence, 142

Dangling modifiers, 88

Dashes, 107

Direct addresses, 99

Direct objects, 39

Direct quotations, 100

Ellipsis marks, 123

Emphasis, 140

Exclamation points, 103

Fragments, 64

Fused (run-on) sentences, 67

Gerunds, 50

Hyphens, 108

Indirect objects, 40

Infinitives, 54

Initialisms (periods with), 126

Interjections, 35

Intransitive verbs, 21

Italics (or underlining), 120

Misplaced modifiers, 87

Mood, 23

Nouns, 4

Noun clauses, 48

Numbers (numerical or spelled), 121

Omissions of letters and words, 99

Parallel structure, 58

Parentheses, 104

Participles and participial phrases, 52

Parts of speech, 4

Passive voice, 22

Periods, 102

Possessives, 113

Predicate adjectives, 37

Predicate nominatives, 38

Prepositions, 31

Pronoun, 5

Pronoun-antecedent agreement, 76

Pronouns case, 79

Punctuation, 90

Questions (structure), 42

Question marks, 103

Quotation marks, 105

Run-on sentences, 69

Semi-colons, 101

Sentence options, 58

Sentence patterns, 37

Sentence problems, 64

Slashes, 106

Squinting modifiers, 84

Subject-verb agreement, 68

Tag questions, 99

Tenses, 16

Transitional phrases, 35

Transitive verbs, 21

Vague pronoun reference, 85

Verbals, 50

Verbs, 14

Word functions, 2

Made in the USA
Middletown, DE
18 October 2018